5 GEARS

How to Be Present and Productive
When There is Never
Enough Time

JEREMIE KUBICEK   STEVE COCKRAM

WILEY

Published by John Wiley & Sons, Inc., Hoboken, New Jersey.
Published simultaneously in Canada.

For general information about our other products and services, please contact our Customer Care Department within the United States at (800) 762-2974, outside the United States at (317) 572-3993, or fax (317) 572-4002.

Wiley publishes in a variety of print and electronic formats and by print-on-demand. Some material included with standard print versions of this book may not be included in e-books or in print-on-demand. If this book refers to media such as a CD or DVD that is not included in the version you purchased, you may download this material at http:// booksupport.wiley.com. For more information about Wiley products, visit www.wiley.com.

Library of Congress Cataloging-in-Publication Data:

Kubicek, Jeremie.
    5 gears : how to be present and productive when there is never enough time / Jeremie Kubicek, Steve Cockram.
        pages cm
    Includes index.
    ISBN 978-1-119-11115-3 (hardback); ISBN 978-1-119-11116-0 (ebk); ISBN 978-1-119-11117-7 (ebk)
    1. Leadership. 2. Interpersonal relations. 3. Self-actualization (Psychology) I. Cockram, Steve. II. Title. III. Title: Five gears.
    HD57.7.K8154 2015
    650.1–dc23   2015013433

Printed in the United States of America.

10 9 8 7 6 5 4 3 2 1

*Jeremie dedicates this book to Kelly,
Addison, Will, and Kate. You four make life amazing.
Thank you for being for me as I am for you.*

*Steve dedicates this book to Helen, Izzy,
Megan, and Charlie.
Thank you for your incredible patience and love
as I've slowly learned how to connect more effectively
with each of you.*

Contents

Introduction

"You're here, but you're really not here. You are with me, but you're somewhere far away." Have you ever heard those words before? Or possibly spoken them to someone else?

Every day, millions of people are negatively impacted by the inability of a person to connect appropriately and to be present. Social miscues, the lack of emotional intelligence, and busyness stifle the growth of people and the progress of organizations.

Additionally, millions of people suffer the consequences of divorce or abuse because people close to them have never learned how to properly connect with one another.

Whether from a boss or a co-worker or a family member, people put up with far too much drama because one person doesn't understand how to shift gears and become present.

Being present is an art form. People can actually learn how to connect well. While some people are naturally good at it, others struggle mightily. Yet those who practice can become masters at being in the right gear at the right time. These are people who know themselves and lead themselves and benefit from the influence and respect that follows.

We are tired of seeing people run over others, tired of dads and moms not being present with their children. We consistently see the disconnections of bosses from those they lead and the lack of awareness that comes from busy adults married to their tasks and missing the point and their lives.

These behaviors are precisely why we have written this book. The world is going through unparalleled cultural upheaval right now and we want to provide practical solutions that transform behavior in adults who have begun to become self-aware of their disconnected lives and trade them in by learning the art of being present.

Relational intelligence is the future competitive advantage for leaders. In the new world the capacity to establish, develop, and maintain key relationships both inside and outside your organization is going to become the primary currency of leadership influence. Relationships are more important than ever.

Be honest about your relational reality.

- Do you know what it's like to be on the other side of you?
- Do you know how to connect with people in every social context?
- Are you easy to connect with in your work setting?
- Do people like being around you?
- Are you able to be physically and emotionally present with people even when you have tight deadlines?

- Do you always have to win?
- Have you truly ever experienced being present with someone else?
- Do you know how to slow down enough to hear what someone else is saying?

These are the questions that will differentiate the leaders of the future. IQ and hard skills are essential but they are no longer enough. When you learn to grow your relational competency—the ability to connect with others and be present—then you will be able to build long-term relationships and obtain a world of opportunity that most will miss.

5 Gears is a power book. It has the power to, if implemented, literally transform the relationships of those you love the most and help you become a significant leader at work and in your community. It is a simple but deep metaphor that is sticky, practical, and usable, *if* you take the time to insert the language and use the system in all five circles of influence—personal, family, team, organization, and community.

IF. If you can admit to the areas in your life where you tend to disconnect and if you are willing to deal with them, then you are on your way. If you are willing to acknowledge your lack of presence in the lives of those around you, and if you're willing to reorder your days to become significant through the power that lies with the 5 Gears, transformation will be yours.

This resource will help you:

- Learn how to be present in the lives of those you live with or lead

- Learn how to shift gears in order to connect well
- Increase your influence as you become more self-aware about yourself and others
- Create a system for communication in teams, families, and organizations
- Eliminate drama that comes from busy lives and self-absorption
- Experience peace because you are engaged, connected, and present

We believe that the emotionally relevant and relationally connected person has a competitive advantage over others simply because the socially awkward, relationally disconnected person misses so much opportunity in their everyday task-driven world.

Our goal is to help you fully experience the joys of leading and living well. We hope to help you become significant and memorable in all areas of your life, and we have created a metaphor and a concept called the 5 Gears that we are using and sharing with thousands of people around the world. The metaphor is based on a manual stick-shift transmission, with each gear correlating to a corresponding behavior that people shift into at certain times and with certain people. The goal of the metaphor is to help you create a language with actual symbols that are used to change the way you live and lead.

Is this a leadership book? Yes. However, it is more than that. It is a book for everyone. We have found that this book is as helpful for the stay-at-home mom who wants more for her family as it is for the professional woman trying to balance work and life. This system is as powerful for the busy executive who desires to manage work–life balance issues as it is for students and youth desiring to become the leaders of the future.

The 5 Gears concept was born out of our own failures and strengths. The very idea was created out of observation: Why do we do what we do? Why, at times, would Jeremie have a hard time personally recharging or staying focused long enough to complete a task? Or why would Steve shift into work mode and miss the opportunity to connect fully with someone he is meeting with?

In our own business, GiANT Worldwide, we began to apply this concept regularly to help the leaders we were serving reconnect with their families, or to help them create a new language to handle work–life balance, or to give them a system to become more effective with their teammates at work. Simply put, we have taken our own inability to connect well or be present and have created a new language and a system that will allow you to experience the same breakthroughs that we, along with thousands of leaders, have experienced.

To give you a taste of what could happen we thought it best to share a story of how 5 Gears has impacted the life of an HR executive named Heather, and how it continues to help her create a language and system for growth, both at work and at home. Though some of the vocabulary in this story may seem unfamiliar at first, we are laying the groundwork for your own personal revelation by showing you right away how the 5 Gears leads to transformation. Her words will define and describe what could happen to you in all your relationships when you implement the ideas in this book into your life.

My name is Heather and I want to share the story of how the 5 Gears has helped me make a really critical discovery about myself, something that should have been common sense but wasn't. I was failing to spend much time in 1st gear/recharge and 2nd gear/connect in my life. No wonder I have been so tired and frustrated! And no wonder I gained back the 50 pounds I lost back in 2010! I wasn't taking the necessary time for me. I was operating mostly in 4th gear/task and 5th gear/focus mode in all circles of influence and in all situations and circumstances.

This tool has changed my life! It allowed me the opportunity to really take a long look in the mirror to see what it has been like to be on the other side of me. I'm a wife, a mother to two young daughters (ages five and eight), a daughter, a friend, an executive, a community member, a Christian, and a board member, to name a few roles. I found myself pretty constantly operating in 4th and 5th gears in each of these roles. The result, aside from being completely exhausted, was that I was failing to really connect with the people in my life—especially my family. I realized this and took accountability for it. No wonder my marriage was falling apart. No wonder my husband didn't even want to hear about my day or my work. No wonder my kids were bored and starting to act out. *I wasn't connecting with them*. And I didn't even realize it! But, after being introduced to this tool, I had the ability to make that realization and know myself, to better lead myself so that I could change my tendencies, which changed my behaviors and, ultimately, changed reality . . . especially for my family.

In the corporate world, we are conditioned to work excessive hours and be accessible 24/7/365. This tool helped me to connect to others in healthy ways, and to disconnect appropriately from work. In fact, it's unhealthy to not disconnect. So, after making this discovery (actually during the Liberating Leader Tour in October 2014), I decided to make some small, but substantial changes in my life. For example, when I leave work, once I get in my car, I turn off email on my phone. It does not go back on until I arrive at work in the morning. I'm not that important. I don't need to respond to messages at all hours of the day and night. Do you want to know what happened? It's the strangest thing! I get far fewer messages in the evenings and on weekends now. Without knowing it, I had actually conditioned our teams to contact me anytime they felt like it . . . because I would always reply! Now, if there is an urgent issue out of normal business hours, they know to call me. Otherwise, they know that I will respond to messages during working hours. Of course there are exceptions when, based on workload or urgent situations, I work in the evening or on the weekend . . . but now, I get my family's permission first!

It has been a liberating realization and experience for me. And the best part is knowing that this is perfectly acceptable. How can I have work–life balance if I'm always accessible, always checking messages, and always responding? I can't! I have the 5 Gears hanging on my wall . . . at work and at home. It's a reminder for me and gives those around me a way to call me out when I need it by simply using language and holding up 1 or 2 whenever I need to shift into the right gear. Thank you for introducing this powerful metaphor!

5 Gears is for you to use in the radical transformation of your relationships, time, and leadership. Once you read it, come back to this story and then add your own at

www.5gears.me. We have created this link for you to share your transformation from being disconnected to connected, socially unaware to aware, and distant to present.

We hope you read our book with the expectation that certain frustrations about yourself or others can be overcome. We believe that you can experience a breakthrough that is profound, and, when you do, we hope you will teach the 5 Gears to everyone that you impact. Give a copy to others, and set up a system of new language that is relevant in your family or organization.

In the end we cannot wait to read your story of transformation and relational connection as you move to a new level of leadership and living.

SECTION ONE

Connectivity

1 | Driving Too Fast

A hard-charging, 40-year-old executive was leaving work, late again. For weeks, his wife had requested that he try to make it home for a hot meal with their three kids before the children got ready for bed. The request didn't seem too unreasonable, but for some reason it was very difficult for the CEO husband to be consistent with this basic level of commitment during this period of his life.

The husband was leading a national company that had a lot of moving parts, employees, and investors. Outside of the normal business he was also in the middle of a possible acquisition, while at the same time working on divesting a portion of the company. Needless to say, his mind was elsewhere for months, as he juggled calls with attorneys and partners, while also managing the day-to-day.

On many occasions the husband would text his wife to say he was on his way home, which was partially true. His stall tactic was pulling in to his neighborhood swim/tennis parking lot to finish up his phone calls before making the final 500 feet to his house. The texts would keep piling in from his wife, "Where are you?" His "almost there" reply made him feel as if he was being truthful. But it was her inevitable, frustrated response, "We are eating without you," that prompted him to end the call with the attorney, pull into his driveway and make his way inside, always with an apologetic monologue to his family and a shoulder shrug to his wife. "It's been crazy busy," he would casually mutter.

The problem is that this event was not a one-time occurrence; it was becoming a habit, or rather a pattern. His über-patient wife was sincere in her desire to simply be together for at least an hour or so a day, since life's schedule had been equally crazy for her with their three children. As the husband grabbed his plate with haste, the comment from his wife made him shudder—"We need to talk!"

Dinner was not pleasant as the busy father faked his way through the conversation with the kids, while juggling thoughts of a possible tiff with his wife, along with the continued pressures of the work that needed to be completed that evening.

Once the kids were down for the night, the guilty husband staggered into their sitting room with a soft-spoken, "Hey," to his irritated but persistent wife.

"This has got to stop," she started. "Every single night I feel as if I am battling with you to simply be consistent. You tell me you will be home at a certain time and then it changes," she shared. "Why is it so hard to do what you say you are going to do?"

Hearing that last comment hurt the husband. She was definitely right. He would tell her he would be home at one time and then miss it completely. In his mind, he would apologize and promise to do better, which was his pattern. She continued to plead her case, as this appetizer of facts was setting the tone for the entrée of frustration and truth telling.

As he began to respond with a litany of excuses, she held up her hand and said, "Wait." Time seemed to slow and it threw the husband for a loop as his mind raced to think about what to say next. She continued, "The real issue is this. When you are with us, you are not *really* with us. It's like work is consuming you, and you never turn off."

"Ouch!" he thought.

"Do you know that when you are with the kids, they are only getting the obligated father-talk version of you? You're going through the motions, doing what you are supposed to do, but not engaging with them, with the *real* you." She spoke this truth clearly and emphatically. She was being honest with her tone and words in order to state the reality with hopes of a deep conversation that would lead to a change in their family dynamics.

He knew she was right, but most men do not want to feel scolded. While his first internal thought was, "I know, you are so right," his defensiveness and pride supplanted any attempt to respond to her frustrations with remorse. He felt judged and misunderstood as thoughts began to emerge in his head: "She doesn't know how much I have on my plate. Doesn't she know how hard I am working to provide for the family?"

His mind caused him to not be present for the last half of her diatribe. He knew he had hurt her, but his irrational mind began creating a defensive wall, and soon he began to lob an emotional tirade back to her to justify his actions.

"Do you really not know what I have been doing?" he jabbed. "I have been working my tail off on an acquisition that could change our life forever. Don't you realize what this could mean for our family?" He went on like a defense lawyer, stating, "I need your support, not your judgment. It feels like you are not here for me." The husband did his best to counter her argument with a personal attack to cause her to retract her statements.

What it caused, instead, were tears. She walked away wounded, as her hopes for responsiveness from her husband were discarded and replaced with embellishment and irrational arguments. The husband paced around his home office steaming, as he tried to justify his words. A feeling of deep regret settled over him as he realized the pain he had inflicted. In his heart, he knew that he was an idiot and that she was right, but he used the moment to defend himself instead of solving the issue.

Does any of this sound familiar to you? Any of you ever experienced this first hand?

I know this story well, because this defensive, pride-filled CEO/husband was actually me (Jeremie), and I am at times a master of turning my wife's truth into needless drama.

What I should have said was, "Wow, I am so sorry. I know that I have promised to be home on time, but I keep missing my mark." That would have soothed some of the frustration. If I had communicated correctly and honestly, she would have heard me continue with this: "I know that my mind has been stuck on work a lot lately. There is just so much going on with the acquisition and divestiture. Honestly, I really need help.

I feel overwhelmed and could use your voice in my life to help me think through all of this and plan our days and my work more effectively."

That, my friends, would have turned an irritated wife into a helpful partner. Instead, I turned a frustrated wife into a frustrated, exasperated wife! Not good.

Running People Over

The episode I just recounted is indicative of most leaders and married couples that I know. Can you relate?

Miscommunication exponentially grows with busy lives, the consumption of technology, the pressures of work, and the desires and expectations of raising healthy families or having good friendships. And these issues are not only synonymous with married couples. Most adults I know struggle with managing tasks, friends, family, and personal entertainment. Each of you could surely add your own story either personally or stories from others in your life or business and how difficult it has been to stay connected and be truly present.

It is not that we want to run people over, and yet we often do. We drive 50 miles an hour in a 20 mile-an-hour speed zone without being aware. People tend to be consumed by schedules and agendas and often run right over those we care about the most. When someone feels the pressure of a deadline or fears the roar of a boss's voice, it is natural to shift focus to alleviating the immediate concern rather than focus on our long-term relationships. The urgent pressure trumps the important relationships most of the time, which tends to steal, kill, and destroy our presence to those we are closest to most of the time.

Conversely, when we are fully present at the right place and right time, those we are with get our best. At our best we can normally meet the needs of those we love, help others with anything they need, and bring health into work cultures or the home. In her appeal, my wife was actually honoring me. She was basically saying, "Jeremie, we love you, but we are not getting the real you. You are amazing with our kids, but work is stealing you away from what we need in our family right now."

I was running over my family because of the pressures of work and the new habits I had formed as it related to work without the ability to turn it off. People run over other people when they are not present or focused on the person or people they are with in the moment. This is where most influence is undermined as people get tired of getting run over. Eventually people move away from those who are not present to others who have more life and less drama.

Social Miscues

Social miscues happen everyday. Do you know that guy who is always on? He wakes up early and sends a few zinger emails to rattle the cages of those he works with? When he gets to the office, instead of offering a "Good morning" to his team, he asks, "Did you get my email?" This is the guy who never turns off at work or at home. And he does not normally realize this fact; he just consistently runs people over with his incessant task-driven approach to life.

"You are talking about me," some of you might say. "You just described my husband," others are thinking.

This is not solely a work issue. We see it every day in social settings as people tire of the social miscues of bosses, co-workers, neighbors, school parents, friends, and family.

What about the person who is always talking about the kids—I mean always. They incessantly share every detail with anyone who is in front of them, focused on the story more than the work. The obviously stuck listener works diligently to lay hints that they need to go without any reception from the child-obsessed talker.

"That is definitely my sister," some of you chuckle. "I know a dozen of these people," others say.

The majority of people are not aware of their social awkwardness and give little time to thinking about what gear the other person is in while they are talking. People don't mean to run each other over, but the truth is that we can all have moments when we are in a different gear than the other person. Our minds can easily get stuck in work mode or kid stories or random thoughts and we can, unknowingly, run others over with our chatter and self-absorption.

Everywhere we look, people show their lack of social competency. Whether it is speaking at the wrong time, failing to listen to those speaking directly to them, or ignoring the most obvious social hints, unawareness is pandemic.

> *We can all have moments of disconnection when we are in a different gear than the other person.*

It usually gets worse in the office environment. Some leaders become different people the moment they walk into an office setting. For some they shift into the "dominator" mode as they bark orders, forget about an employee's birthday, or send emails that would make their mother blush.

Recently I heard a story about a chairman sharing his desire to improve company culture at a board meeting. When another executive began asking some probing questions about his thoughts, the chairman swiveled and responded in absolute terms that no one should question his authority to get things accomplished. His tantrum was preposterous to everyone but the chairman. The executive had just been blasted in front of all the others. You could see the singe marks on his suit as his blushing cheeks showed his embarrassment. The rest of the executives went back into hiding in their shells of protection to make sure that never happened to them.

Whether it is a young teenager behind a register talking on a cell phone to a friend at work, or one family member asking awkward questions to another, social miscues are embarrassing and infuriating and cause disconnection.

You can actually sit in an airport or a restaurant or an office and find dozens of examples of social awkwardness. While some people are truly born with social and relational dysfunction, others are simply either lazy or too busy to stop and notice. Lazy people have given up on self-improvement, personal growth, or relational connectivity. That leaves the majority completely unaware because they are in too much of a hurry to stop, analyze, and change. When a person's agenda is the driving force of their life, then they are going to run over people most of the time unless they learn to use their brakes and downshift.

Disconnections

This social behavior creates disconnections, which lead to the consequences of fighting, discord, and an overall lack of harmony in relationships, both personally and professionally. All of these issues cost organizations and people as these disconnections breed drama and frustration. So what causes these disconnections and how can you avoid them? Why do some people have the ability to connect while others have the distinction of being disconnected most of the time?

The guy who walks up to you in a social setting but looks beyond you to find out who else is in the room. That is a disconnection. What about the woman who is constantly hinting at something without stating her true expectations? That is a disconnection.

Humans crave connectivity. We have to have it in order to thrive and exist, regardless of introversion or extroversion. And though we desire to be connected, we have certain life experiences, hardwiring in our personalities, and histories of personal choices that have shaped our ability to connect appropriately or otherwise struggle through painful disconnection.

Connectivity is about time, settings, people, places, and motive. It is not as simple as being somewhere physically, but is a combination of emotions, physical connection, spiritual cognizance, and mental aptitude. This understanding is a practical view of improving the quality of our lives and leadership through the art and science of connectivity.

Connectivity is directly related to peace, productivity, and personal happiness.

When you connect deeply with someone, there is such a peace of mind and sense of gratitude that occurs. And to have this type of connection, you and I must learn how to be still and present in the moment. Conversely, when we disconnect we oftentimes do not realize it unless someone confronts us, which tends to bring up defensive pride in the same way it did with me in communicating with my wife. Therefore, one person can experience deep joy most days because they are intentional and aware of their connectivity, while another person goes along on their way wondering why people won't respond to them or acted funny at their last meeting.

Social disconnections affect relational dynamics in all phases of life. I am amazed how many people live in social quagmires with others. People seem to have uncanny tolerance for dysfunctional relationships—allowing family members or close friends to get away with despicable actions in order to "keep the peace." This happens often in the work environment where a high-performing employee is not held accountable to socially acceptable behavior because they are a valued contributor either financially or intellectually. Connectivity is directly related to peace, productivity, and personal happiness.

Let's take a connectivity inventory here to ask ourselves where we currently are when it comes to emotional intelligence and relational connectivity:

- How are your relationships right now with your family (spouse, kids, siblings, or parents)? Are you connecting with them, running over them, or disengaging entirely?
- Do you have friends that you are pouring into by adding value to their lives or if we interviewed them would they tell us that you are consumed with your agenda/schedule and simply put up with you because they are loyal?

- How connected are you to those you work with? Do they spend time and energy to work or walk around you or are you socially connected to them in a healthy way?
- Do you feel like you have the capability to be present with people or are you consumed with social media and other distractions?

The majority of people don't want to run over other people, but it has simply become commonplace. Patterns are created because there are no checks or balances in the lives of busy leaders. We need others who are willing to hold up the mirrors to show us what it is like to be on the other side of ourselves. If we are not connected, please, someone, tell us.

The key is to know yourself, your tendencies and patterns, so that you can lead yourself to act in a manner worthy of your values and to meet the needs of those around you for their benefit as well as yours. Instead of running people over, not being present, and disconnecting we are going to help you establish a new way of living, leading, and connecting.

Before we get to the solution, though, it is important to understand the implications of living a life where your speeds are unchecked and where people are being run over every day. We really want you to see the consequences of your actions when you are not present with those most important to you, and the ramifications of not being aware of your social miscues and your rampant disconnection and how that affects your work, your organizations, and friends or family. Only then will you get to a place where you can truly change.

If you can take a good look in the mirror, vis-à-vis this book, and see that you have broccoli in your teeth, then maybe we can convince you, and help you, to take it out yourself. When people begin to see that you are working on yourself, to become someone that others want to follow, not someone they have to follow, then they will begin to respect you in new ways. Your influence will expand and you will begin to see that people will pull from you instead of run from you.

Our goal is to help you not hit a wall in your relationships, but rather help you have a real breakthrough that will change the way that you interact with others for the rest of your life.

2 | ⚙

Reality Check

So, let's get to your reality. Do people really know you? Would they say that you are normally present with them or constantly in your own world? It is time to get real and honest with your ability, or lack thereof, to connect with others, to be present with them, and to be able to balance work and life in a meaningful way.

Reality, according to dictionary.com, is "the world or the state of things as they actually exist, as opposed to an idealistic or notional idea of them." Therefore, to get to reality, one has to verbalize the actual state of things by admitting what does and does not exist.

Personally, I have a hard time connecting with people who are not interested in global ideas or in talking about philosophic concepts. That is a fact, and it's a reality for me. The consequence of this is that at times I can quietly shut down or become disinterested if I perceive someone to be boring or small-minded. That sounds harsh in writing, but it is so true. That is my reality check: If I am not careful, I can look like a prima donna around ideas on leadership or culture change and the like.

Steve Cockram is the cofounder of GiANT Worldwide and codeveloper of the 5 Gears concept. I love to hear Steve describe his reality check when his in-laws took his family on a cruise to Belgium. Hear his reality below:

My wife's parents gifted us with a vacation to celebrate their anniversary. Helen and I, along with our three girls, boarded the cruise ship with mixed emotions. My family was excited about the time away as it had been a while since we had had a true vacation. While I was excited about it, I was also a bit tense as we had so much business happening in the UK at the time. You see, my reality at the time was that my cell phone was attached to me at all times—almost tethered, to be more descript. I was constantly on with text messages, email conversations, and phone calls. Add to that the fact that I really love watching my cricket and seeing if Liverpool won or not.

As we walked onto the gangplank aboard the ship I had already decided that I would be able to get some emails knocked out and maybe a few calls while everyone else experienced all of the activities the ship had to offer. All was good while still anchored at harbor, as I was able to send a few emails, make some final requests, and check in on a few sports scores simultaneously.

The problem came as the ship left the sight of land as my Wi-Fi coverage dissipated. As I checked into the Wi-Fi options on the ship I realized that they were very proud of their Wi-Fi coverage. They offered me service equal to a small fortune on a per-hour rate, which, if you know me, was not going to happen. When I shared this catastrophic issue with my wife, Helen, she gave me that look that conveyed, "Really Steve?!" Her suggestion was simple as she stated my new reality. "The only thing to do is lock the phone in the safe and enjoy the vacation."

She was so right. We had the best vacation I have ever had. I couldn't do anything and I didn't have work that couldn't wait a few days. I was forced to be present with my family, which brought to light the fact that I truly do like my family, not just love them. They are amazing young girls and my wife is brilliant. I know myself well enough to know that if I had had the phone then I would have been preoccupied with scores, emails, and social media and would have missed my family.

My eldest daughter, Izzy, described the reality that I am addicted to my phone the best by sharing a comment that went right to the heart. She said, "Dad, this was the best vacation I have ever had. It is amazing what happens when your phone doesn't distract you. I love you!"

Ouch! My reality is that I am addicted to my phone and all that it holds and that addiction keeps me distant and distracted on occasion with those I love the most.

Now it is your turn: Take a moment to think about your reality. If I were to ask those closest to you, what would they say about your reality? Would it sound like this?

- "Don just never turns off. He is always on and, while I like him, I can only handle small doses of him."
- "Todd is always joking around. It's like life is a bar. He just hangs out and never seems to get engaged in real work."

- "Amy is tense. I keep telling her to take time for herself, but she has to take care of everyone else first and then never ends up making time for her."
- "John is so talented but always keeps to himself. I would love to get to know him but he is either working with his office door closed or he has left to go run or work out. It's just hard to get to know him."
- "Sarah seems to be a great mom, but I can never get her to talk about anything other than her kids. They seem great, but she doesn't ask me any questions—ever. It is always about her and her kids."

Disconnections! Poor self-awareness. Not being present. Which one of these is most like you? What is your reality?

Before we get started here on a solution to help you connect more vibrantly with others and to increase your influence and your leadership abilities, we want you to explore a few of these powerful questions with the hopes that they may break up some unawareness and lead to a productive and level foundation to build upon instead of you hitting a wall.

Try to answer as many as you possibly can or highlight them to spend time answering in the near future.

1. **What are your priorities?** If someone looked deeply into your life, could they see what your priorities truly are? This is not to judge, but simply to get to reality. Is it sports, money, family, faith, health? What are they in order? And are they what they should be? Align your priorities with your life and with those in your life and watch the relational connectivity improve almost overnight.

2. **When do you tend to run people over?** Is it at work when it happens or is it at home with your family? Why

do you think it is happening? Lastly, do you even recognize it is happening?

3. **Is there a character issue in your life that is causing you to disconnect or disengage?** For many leaders, there is a secret character issue that continues to undermine them. Face it. Tell one person you trust about it so that it can come out into the light and stop letting that issue boss you around.

4. **Is there one relationship that needs to be made right?** Every one of us has a relationship that is not working. So far as it depends on you, how can you try to bring resolution to that person? Write that person down, make a plan, and decide when you will address the relational issue face-to-face.

5. **Where has your influence declined?** At work or at home, is your influence diminishing? Ask yourself if those people believe that you are for them, or do they think that you are for yourself or against them? Determine to fight for their highest possible good and be brave enough to face it.

6. **What are you afraid of losing?** Is it salary, control, respect, time, and so on? When you face your fear it will have less control over you. Oftentimes these fears cause us to strain and stress to a degree that we run over others.

7. **Do people want to follow you or simply have to follow you?** Ouch, this one could hurt. When you realize that people don't really want to follow you, but do so in order to keep their jobs or have to because they live in your house as a dependent, it is painful. I want to be someone that people want to follow and have realized there are things that make it hard for them to do that. Let's fix that.

8. **When do you start working?** Do you wake up and begin to check your email as the very first thing? Have

you noticed how this affects relationships, your mindset, and the rest of the day?

9. **Do you recharge well at home?** If you work from home or lead kids, are there any intentional breaks or times to recharge or is everything simply one big task list? Do you manage your schedule appropriately or has it gotten out of control?

10. **Do you get quality time with others?** When you get time with others are you able to disconnect your task world and connect with the person you are with appropriately? When was the last time you had a meaningful connection with someone else?

11. **Would others say that you know them?** At work, do you know what is going on in the personal lives of those you work with? Would they say you did?

12. **What is the reality of your meetings?** When you have a meeting do you try to connect personally before getting into the task at hand?

13. **What is your demeanor when you come home?** Do you tend to come home later than others expect at night? Is this a habit like it was for me?

Disconnections, poor self-awareness, or the lack of being present—which one of these is most like you?

Write down your thoughts. Talk to someone who knows you well about some of your answers. The goal here is to help you get to your reality, see yourself in a mirror, and begin to increase your influence on those you lead. By doing so you may have just started the process of reconciliation or personal peace, or you may see an uptick in productivity as you address the issues that make your realities unsustainable.

Pain of the Crash

You have heard my story—the pain of disconnecting and hurting my wife in the process. The truth is that most people live in the pain of not being present and the unintended consequences of being unaware of our social disconnects.

The key here is for you and me to first become aware. Most people simply don't know what they don't know. Once they do, there is pain in the progress of realizing that they have been doing things that may be hurting others without that intention. So, let me warn you that in this process you may experience pain. For instance, how present or connected are you with:

- Your parents if they are still alive?
- Your spouse?
- Your children?
- Your boss?
- Your friends?
- Your co-workers?

When you become aware of what you don't do well, you can naturally begin to beat yourself up for your lack of awareness. I just met with a president of a mid-sized firm who realized that he is still acting like a single guy in his marriage. He has been married for 10 years! Therefore, his reality hit him with the pain he has caused his wife and he was thrust right in the middle of his conscious incompetence. He began being flooded with other realities surrounding how that affected his kids, parents, friends, and so on. His wife is frustrated and he is working to get around the corner to become consciously competent at being a husband after years of living as a single guy.

Another executive we have worked with runs a small business in the Midwest that has done quite well over time. When you meet this man you can see his drive and intensity. He has worked hard to build something that benefits the people in his community and his family. While he is respected in his community and organization, no one wants to be around him because he never turns off. He keeps running his people over because his "thinker," as he calls it, is always thinking.

When he experienced the 5 Gears, he realized why people literally try to avoid him in the halls and why he is rarely invited to social gatherings in the community. His intensity is, well, intense. In trying to understand him it became clear that he doesn't value social settings and views them as a waste of time. His kids are gone and his wife has her own business and so he does what he does—works—all the time. After hearing some of the comments from his team and how they see him as a dominator when he sees himself as a liberator, there was great frustration knowing that he makes others' lives miserable.

Our solution was simple. Understand the natural time of the day and what people need at those times. We encouraged him to understand the need for social time and how his wiring was radically different from his employees'. He is still proc-essing his reality now that he sees it. It is up to him to start the process of implementing change in himself first.

Pain can be a good thing. The body creates a fever to fight off infection. Pain itself is meant to bring attention to an issue in the body. Therefore, if you are feeling pain in an area, run toward it because it might be the area that needs some focus. Remember, we are trying to get you to conscious competence, but it could take years to get to that level, as all good things take time to develop and practice.

What we are trying to get away from is the social unawareness that comes with busy, self-absorbed, or emotionally unintelligent people. We are trying to help you avoid these issues:

- People stop getting excited to see you.
- People ignore you or, worse, hide from you.
- People do not spend time with you anymore.
- People cannot trust you with their deepest issues.
- Jokes get made about you and they feel personal.
- Your kids stop getting excited that you are home because you are not happy to be there.

Let's get a really good look at reality, deal with the pain that comes with it, and move into productive living and leading.

What Could Be?

Let's finish up this chapter with an imagination exercise. Imagine the best season possible with your spouse or someone who you care about deeply. The two of you are consistently on the same page, communicating easily. Picture yourself being appreciated and being present with that person enough to really value what they are excited about. There are few distractions and your time becomes exactly what you have always hoped it could be.

Now, picture your kids, if you have any. Visualize them respecting you, and your being able to speak to them with love and appreciation. You may not be as far away as you think you are.

Last one. Imagine that you are at work and those on your team or organization value you at the highest levels they can. Your influence has grown dramatically all because you have learned how to be present at the right time, in the right way, and with your emotional intelligence firing on all cylinders.

This could be you! You could experience the highest levels of relational capital that you have had to date. If you implement the 5 Gears, then you might just be able to regain the lost capital from years of neglect, self-absorption, or busyness. However, it will require a lifestyle change.

We have worked hard over the years to produce tools that are simple, scalable, and sustainable. In the text up to this point we have tried to state the case for why you should be present and to help you understand the pain caused when you are disconnected or socially unaware. It is now time to begin to learn the language that shifts realities and marks a new course for effective leadership and dynamic relationships. It's time to get in gear.

SECTION TWO

5 Gears for Practical Connection

3 | ⚙

Getting in Gear

Think about your first car. Some of you can close your eyes and envision when your eyes first gazed upon it. You were entranced, as you longed to be able to drive like an adult. It is amusing to hear how adults describe their first vehicle, especially if it had unique qualities. Even if the car was a junker, there were certain things that stood out to you.

Remembering your first car is one thing; remembering how you first drove that vehicle is a completely different memory. Some of you started with a vehicle with a manual stick shift. Do you remember what those first few drives were like? The grinding gears and jerky ride as you tried hard to manage the clutch and accelerator while attempting to stay on the road. If you don't remember, I am sure those who rode with you do.

Driving is difficult, with all of the inputs and decisions that need to be made. The same goes with leadership. Communicating a vision, managing people, dealing with issues, all as you try to stay focused on your own personal tasks and goals can be quite difficult. Leading well is similar to driving well. Over time you get in a rhythm if you observe and practice, but those first few years can be tense to say the least.

My first car was a 1972 Alfa Romeo GT2000. It was a sleek, candy-apple red, two-door, five-speed beauty. As a 16-year-old living in a small city in central Oklahoma, it felt as James Bond-ish as any car could. The windshield wipers alternated toward one another and the smooth lines along the small car gave it a very distinct, European feel. The crown jewel of my beautiful new, old car, however, was the elegant wood. The steering wheel was made from a distinguished walnut wood, as was the manual gearshift handle.

As a new driver who was getting acclimated to a manual transmission, that poor car had to deal with my grinding gears and timid use of the clutch. I had to practice shifting, learning to listen to the engine to know when to shift, and then practicing a smooth transition from one gear to the next.

As I became a bit more confident in my driving skills, I remember trying to start driving straight out of second gear while avoiding first gear altogether. Starting in first just took too long and I had places to go, people to see, things to do. I thought I could just skip a gear and get to fourth or fifth gear as fast as possible. That was a mistake. It didn't take long before I learned what such impatience did to the engine, not to mention my plummeting gas mileage, and the lurching effect it caused.

Twenty-plus years later I found myself living in the English countryside, staring at a right-sided steering wheel and a left-handed manual stick shift in our first rental car. Learning to drive on what the English call the correct side of the road is one thing. But adding a left-handed gear shift to the equation made driving on the opposite side of the road even more challenging, given how intently I had to focus on shifting as we drove on the tiny lanes of London. I would sum up the experience with the following words: Grinding gears, close calls, lurching motions, and terror—I mean, excitement.

There are parallels with shifting gears in a car and the rhythms and routines of our lives: There is a right order and a right time for each gear. Conversely, there is also a wrong gear and a wrong time. People who figure this out tend to drive smoothly and effectively. People who don't shift well tend to cause damage to all those around them—people and vehicles.

There is a right time and a right place for each gear.

1st gear is meant to lead to 2nd and so forth. Each gear has a purpose, and if you understand the purpose and apply this driving analogy to the way you "drive" your life, aligning the right gear with the right speed and situation of your day will allow you to have a smooth journey. Conversely, if you choose to skip a gear, as in my example, then you may rev to screaming levels and cause the engine of your life all sorts of problems.

The 5 Gears is a metaphor centered on an everyday, manual transmission vehicle or stick shift. Most European cars have a manual gearbox, while most American vehicles have an automatic transmission. In both cases there are gears that start in 1st gear and shift through until you reach 5th gear (unless you drive a very expensive car that adds a 6th gear). Reverse is also a gear, which could make up a 6th or 7th gear depending on the car, but for simplicity we will use 5 Gears as the overall theme of the metaphor.

With our metaphor, each gear represents a different mode of connecting through living, leading, working, and resting. We will define each one and give concrete examples throughout to help make this a practical system for connectivity, work–life balance, and to improve emotional intelligence.

To start, let's look at the gear order as you see it in Figure 3.1. 1st gear leads to 2nd, which leads to 3rd, and so on.

Figure 3.1   5 Gears

The same thinking applies to our metaphor: To lead yourself well and connect appropriately in your relationships, your day needs to begin in 1st gear, after which you shift up into other gears. You can go from 1st gear to 5th in life, but it is not recommended and the consequences can be damaging, just like with your car. You can also go from 3rd gear to reverse, but just because you can, does not mean you should, considering cause and downstream effect. The best drivers understand when to shift and when not to. The same is true with the best leaders. They understand the gears.

- 1st gear represents being fully recharged.
- 2nd gear represents connecting with family, friends, or colleagues.
- 3rd gear is the social gear.
- 4th gear is the task gear that allows us to work hard while also multitasking.
- 5th gear is focus mode that allows us to "get in the zone" without interruption.
- Reverse is the responsive gear. It is used when we need to back up and start again or apologize.

Each gear has its own purpose and place. Once you learn to use the gears consistently with those in your life, you will notice the common language that begins to form, enabling objectivity to characterize your conversation instead of the subjective judgment or condescension that becomes pervasive when each person is speaking a different "language." With the gears, you will also be able to incorporate some shorthand sign language to describe what gear you are in with a hand signal, which makes conversations more efficient and effective among people who share the same language.

5 GEARS

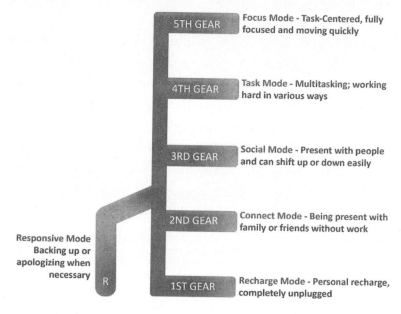

Figure 3.2   The 5 Gears Tool

Without further ado, here are the 5 Gears in a visual form to give you detail and context (Figure 3.2). Many people hang this tool up in their break rooms at work or on their refrigerator at home.

Each one of you has a personal gearbox, 5 Gears, plus reverse, at your disposal to use in your daily life. Some of you already intuitively shift up and down into the right gears with ease, similar to having driven a car for many years, where you no longer have to think about the individual mechanics of going from point A to point B. You are not analyzing your shifting; you just do it.

Others of you are less than competent with regard to the way you are driving your life: You have not been aware that you may be breaking social etiquette or missing relational cues at work or at home. If you are experiencing frustration in any of your relationships, this is a clue as to what category you are currently in. Learning these gears is the key to helping you connect with people in the right way and to eliminate socially awkward situations, and even begin to repair damaged relationships. If you understand how to drive your life with these gears, you will unlock depths of connection and influence in your relationships that you never knew existed.

It took me a few years to master the art of driving a five-speed, eventually shifting the stick shift with ease and grace. It has taken me much longer to learn how to shift the actual relational gears in my life and become consistent. And the progress I have made has not come without constant practice and intentionality in matching my gear to the context of the situation.

In our culture most adults suffer from one or two of three connectivity problems:

1. They rarely understand which gear they are operating in at any given moment.
2. They rarely know what gear the other people in their life are operating in.
3. They rarely take the time to practice shifting and operating in each gear.

This combined lack of awareness and practice explains why we have so many people suffering from the realities of workaholism, social awkwardness, rude commentary, and a rash of disconnection within families, spousal relationships, boards, and teams. Imagine how many marriages have crumbled simply because two people have not learned

how to shift gears or consistently remain emotionally connected. Think about how many employees are fired because

The life of the disconnected person is frustrating for both the individual as well as those around them.

they haven't learned the basics of emotional intelligence and shifting through the 5 Gears.

Healthy and Unhealthy Gears

Each gear in the 5 Gears metaphor has both a healthy and an unhealthy side. Some of us are good at using the gears, while others will tend to abuse them. You might have heard the words of people who have failed to learn how to shift well:

- "I don't understand how they misinterpreted my words. I told them I was . . . ."
- "My wife should know this is a busy season. I have told her how important my work is right now."
- "They don't seem to get me. It is so frustrating."
- "I work hard and play hard. I do put in the hours to be able to serve my family. They understand that I have to work long hours to maintain that."
- "I already know what you are going to say. I don't need to be looking at you to hear you."

The life of the disconnected person is frustrating for both the individual as well as those around them. So you might be wondering: can breakdowns in social dynamics and relational connections be healed through the common language of the 5 Gears? Fortunately, the answer is yes, and here's why: Healthy use of each gear leads to productivity in work, deeper relationships with those we care about, and effective personal recharge within the context of your natural wiring. Unhealthy use of the gears, however, will ultimately cause disconnection in most areas of life—work, home, friendships, and so on.

At the end of each gear chapter we will add a healthy and unhealthy gear application so that you can apply this into your life immediately as you grow to become a leader worth following and implement this language into your culture.

Using Language to Connect

Language can connect people together and it can tear people apart. We know this from being taught as children by parents not to say anything if we cannot be kind, right? The language of 5 Gears can help deliver messages in situations where frustration or distortion is imminent in a way that does not harm others. For instance, if a group of employees is stuck in social mode at work you could use words like, "Let's go! You all are always the last ones, aren't you? We are not running a day care here . . ." Or, if your team speaks 5 Gears, you could hold up a number 4 followed by a simple, "Hey, guys . . ." to the group with a chuckle as your shorthand way to help people shift up from 3rd to 4th gear in the office. Language has the power to heal or kill. When used properly, it can guide people in helping themselves and others.

Here is how L.V. Hanson, a director at a company called Har-Bro, in Southern California, explains the 5 Gears in his world:

The 5 Gears tool has become a game changer for our team. Albert Einstein once said, "If you can't explain it to a

six-year-old, you don't understand it yourself." The beauty
of genius is its simplicity, and 5 Gears is genius . . . because
it's simple. In the art of restoring a leadership language, 5
Gears provides language that transfers simply, quickly, and
relationally . . . and invites solution to potential awkward
or conflict-oriented moments. I have a colleague that will
laugh and ask me to shift to 3rd gear when we are at lunch
and I'm going on and on about a problem at work that I'm
trying to solve. Rather than tell me "shut up" or "gosh, can
you just leave work at work," this friend asks me if I will
shift to 3rd gear—a question that moves through potential
conflict by acknowledging where I am and where I need to
be through one simple, invitational question. He acknowl-
edges that what I'm dealing with is legitimate and important, but that it is a question most appropriately asked in 4th
gear, and rather than criticize me for staying in the wrong
gear, he invites me into 3rd gear . . . into relationship . . .
which is actually what I need most in that moment of stress
and frustration. I never solve problems well when I'm doing
it in stress.

Words matter. Language is shaped on everyone's understanding of what the words mean. When we work to define
the words and practice using the vocabulary, then we have a
better chance of building a significant culture and move more
fervently than getting stuck in drama or insecurity.

A songwriter friend of mine, Don Chaffer, teaches that the
power of writing songs is in the combination of concrete and
abstract language. He claims that the best songs are a mix of
both abstract and concrete words.

The same holds true with the language we use when
leading, directing, or communicating with others. To tell

someone they need to "improve their leadership" is acceptable as an introductory statement, but is abstract in form. It should always be followed by concrete examples and specific language about how the person can improve their leadership.

This is an example of concrete language: "I want you to learn to challenge your team more consistently; you seem to be having trouble holding them accountable for the agreed upon goals," or "at times you get overly emotional in your interactions with this group and are losing your influence as a result." Whatever the leadership issue may be, using abstract language as your primary means of communicating can drive people to cynicism over time and cause them to doubt the effectiveness of your leadership.

Analyze your words. Are you using both abstract and concrete words to communicate your message? Or are you only using the abstract? Language directs people. Language sets a tone. If you want to connect more effectively with others, then watch your language.

The beauty of the 5 Gears is that it provides an objective, concrete language to help people more effectively calibrate their connectivity. Integrating this language into everyday life can help dramatically improve the emotional intelligence of everyone with whom you interact, regardless of age or relationship.

Imagine how nimble and drama free your workplace could be with the simple addition of a precise, common language. A language whose clear objectivity eliminated the subjective ambiguity of the words and concepts that too often give rise to misunderstanding and conflict.

Pat Donovan, an engineer from Florida, has taken this metaphor even further:

Tonight after getting home from work, I was working with my sixth-grade daughter Mia Grace on a school project. During a break we discussed our respective days and I mentioned that one of my highlights was discussing the 5 Gears at our GiANT core group training. I ended up pulling up the 5 Gears graphic and reviewing it with her. She immediately grasped the concept and remarked, "Dad, that's just like in our band class. Some kids really want to learn and are in 5th gear but others are always talking, which is more like 3rd gear. Others want to learn but get distracted by the talkers, which seems like 4th gear." We talked a little about how hard it must be for the band director to try and keep all these different groups focused on the same goal. It was fun and rewarding for the two of us to connect over discussing this concept and share the same language.

Pat goes on to share:

As someone who still drives a car with a standard transmission, I know that it is important to have the car in the right gear for the given driving circumstance or situation. Being in the right gear is event-specific and the car will keep running when you match the gear to the circumstance. There are times driving a car when the circumstances change and you need to downshift to a lower gear. Climbing a hill is a perfect example. The point is to keep the gear selection matched to the circumstance. As long as you do that the car will keep running. Where you get into trouble is when the car is in the wrong gear for the circumstance. Whether it's too high or too low, being in the wrong gear is what will cause damage.

In applying this analogy to work or life, I think these basic concepts are valid; however, the difference is that there is a cumulative effect on the "car" (person) based on the journey. The gears also seem to relate to energy or effort expended and the ups and downs of the journey require a cumulative or total amount of energy to get to the destination efficiently. As such, in life/work, it is important to keep a balance between the gears shifting to ensure you actually get to where you are trying to go. Even though some cars/people might have higher capacity "engines," you still need some kind of gear balance over time to make sure you get there and don't crash.

I love hearing our clients and friends from around the globe share their realities. Pat has truly applied the concept in his everyday world, as well as applying it at home. The same can happen with you. This next section highlights how the 5 Gears can not only add value, but also keep you from the pains of disconnections.

How the 5 Gears Saved an iPhone and Improved a Marriage

Keeping in balance is so difficult in this period of history. Technological advances, social media, entertainment, work, family, and personal time are hard to manage and do well.

Could the 5 Gears actually make technology, entertainment, and social connectivity fit more smoothly in your life? Is it possible to use the 5 Gears to restore relationships and emotional intelligence as you learn to connect with real people in a real way? To both we say yes.

Ryan Underwood, CEO of TRI Leadership Resources, shares how the 5 Gears has worked and is working for him.

As a creative introvert, my 1st gear is spent recharging with my apps, learning, and acquiring knowledge. I have over 700 apps and for every percent of battery I use on my phone, I feel like it personally charges me up. So, when I need to recharge and chill, I do it best with my iPad or iPhone. With technology being so convenient, if there is any momentary pause in the family action, it's easy to whip out my phone and access anything I want and then return to the family action quickly. At least, that's my rationale.

However, my extroverted bride doesn't see it this way. She doesn't see my iPhone as a recharge, but rather as a disrupter, interrupter, and device of rudeness to her, our friends, the girls, and so on. Steve Jobs' beloved device was at one point renamed from the iPhone to the Damn Phone in her vocabulary because of its power over me. It was seen as a black hole to her, where my time, energy, and attention became absorbed and her husband taken away.

Needless to say we had an issue. I dig my data as it helps make me . . . me, and she was growing frustrated at the mere sight of my iPhone. To her it seemed that I'd rather be on my phone than be present and available for her, family, and so on. As you can imagine, we were at a standoff.

That is when we found the 5 Gears, just in time . . . and it saved my iPhone and more importantly improved our marriage (and is setting a better example for our girls who I know will one day be all plugged in and too busy on their phones for Mom and Dad). We both know the language, vocabulary, and what the gears mean. So, now instead of threatening to break the phone, she kindly asks, "What gear are we in?" I receive that question so much better and she gets the response that she wants, which is me saying "2nd gear" and then putting the phone away. No drama or intense marital conversation. We both shift into 2nd gear—present for each other.

Marriage and iPhone rescued!

That is the secret of the 5 Gears. It is a clear concept that uses objective language and practical signals to help us become more present—to be in the right gear at the right time in the right way.

As we extend the metaphor, I think you'll find the gears concept solidifying in your vocabulary. We will continue to expand this vocabulary. We will discuss more about reverse, being in neutral, and how to transition into the right gears at work, home, and in our personal lives as we become healthy and mature leaders and people.

4 | 5th Gear—In the Zone

Have you ever looked up at the clock after working intensely on a project and been amazed at how quickly the time has flown by? That is 5th gear. Some of you love 5th gear. Just the thought of getting in the zone without disruption revs your engines. You can picture yourself at your favorite workstation, completely focused on your task. Just thinking of that special place might cause some of you to put this book down and get back to your hobby or work—it is simply that exciting.

On the other side of the spectrum, though, large majorities of you are not even sure what 5th gear looks like. Maybe you have experienced it once or twice, this idea of being fully absorbed by and engaged in the task at hand to the point that everything in your periphery falls away and all you see is what's in front of you, but you simply haven't mastered the ability to focus for long periods of time and stay in the zone. If this sounds familiar, take heart: you are not alone. Given our propensity to multitask, not to mention the distractions of technology, many of us find it difficult to even find 5th gear, let alone stay in it.

5th gear is focus mode. It is the gear where the ability to hyperfocus and experience the flow of your work becoming something productive is key. To someone watching you operate in 5th gear, you might appear to be in a trance, completely unaware of noises, voices, and the normal distractions that might cause others less focused to shift their attention. When people get in to 5th gear they tend to not need anything other than their work. Even food can wait at times.

Getting into Overdrive

"So, how can I find this gear?" you ask.

A car's engine will tell you when it's time to shift gears—so, too, does your work. It simply takes discipline to shut the door, turn off your email, and let people know that you are shifting into 5th gear—going into overdrive. When you reach this gear, your productivity reaches the highest levels possible.

When a car reaches overdrive the engine is able to maintain a speed at a lower engine level, which allows a car to get better fuel mileage with less wear and tear. If a car needs more power at higher speeds, the overdrive enables it to reach that level.

Can you reach overdrive?

Here are some points that will help you understand the correlation of overdrive to your personal 5th gear.

- A healthy 5th gear makes it possible to cruise at a sustained speed for a period of time.
- Because 5th gear occurs mostly when we are either passionate about our work or simply competent at it, our engine speed is actually lower, while our sustained speed can be quite fast.
- Therefore, less energy is needed to produce quality or high speeds. Focus can lead to high levels of productivity.
- 5th gear can produce great results and high speeds for a period of time. However, people (similar to engines) are not meant to stay in 5th gear all day long.

Some of you get into 5th gear when you do planning for the year or month. Others get into and stay in 5th gear as part of your day job, especially where highly mechanical, creative, technological, or medical fields are concerned: engineers working on designs; IT service professionals finishing a project; machine operators; interior designers; surgeons or dental hygienists. There are certain roles and jobs that lend themselves to 5th gear. For the rest of us, we have to schedule it or focus on it.

For executive leaders, 5th gear can be seen as the strategy gear, when you are working on the business and thinking in the long-term strategic planning zone. This might include dreaming, vision casting, exploring ideas, or thinking of major changes in life, work, or business.

5th gear allows you to get into the zone.

To give you an idea of what this looks like, let me tell you about one of our partners. Jeff is a serial entrepreneur involved in some of the most amazing projects in the United States today and has multiple teams that he oversees on an everyday basis. He is one of the greatest guys I know, always having time for people who need help. He also happens to love 5th gear. Here is how he describes being in 5th gear with one of his developments:

> So, since learning about the 5 Gears, I've been working the gears into my everyday conversations. It has helped articulate my frustration. I live in this 5th gear/overdrive space (strategic thinking). My managers are constantly in 4th gear because of the variety of work they are involved in and they get pulled into business 3rd gear with homeowners. I keep asking them to meet me in 5th gear when I am on-site, but it feels like they can't get there. I only need them in 5th gear with me a couple days a year to define strategic plans for the year. The gears have helped me realize my communication breakdown and how to better communicate with my team so we can be in the same gear at the same time.

With the 5 Gears vocabulary in the water system, Jeff can now describe to his team what he needs and he can also help them to get to that 5th gear with him.

If you identify with Jeff's story, then here are some thoughts for you to consider in helping your teams:

- Set expectations: Before you meet, let them know you are going to set aside a period of time when you want everyone to be in 5th gear together. This will help them prepare mentally to operate in a different gear.
- Hold the gathering off-site, completely away from their normal task world.
- Ask the managers to delegate 4th gear tasks to others back at the office for the duration of your off-site session.

- Ask your managers to set up auto-responder out-of-office emails to ensure that tasks don't disrupt the strategic time.
- Begin the off-site 5th gear time with an exercise that gets your managers thinking about the future, such as having them list five things they would love to see happen in the organization in three years.
- Ask them to give you real thoughts, objections, and insights into the future. Listen to their real issues and give them real time to discuss them.
- Make sure you share your expectations for the kind of feedback you want, and discuss what 5th gear looks like to you.
- Ask them what they need from you during this same period of time.

Remember that the 5 Gears are designed to be a language that people use to shift into the right gear at the right time. More specifically, 5th gear allows you and others to get into the zone at work or with a project at home.

Rethinking the Open Door Policy

For most of us, 5th gear is a personal gear; it's a gear we shift up into when we need to work on our own, think strategically, or be singularly productive with one task. It normally occurs with our personal focus. And yet we all affect each other on each team we are on.

If you have been working inside an organization for any length of time then you have most likely heard the phrase "Open Door Policy." You might have heard it from a boss who brags that he or she always has an open door policy to connect with their employees.

The problem with this "policy" is that it often limits people from being productive when they need to focus. There are times when you need to close the door and other times when you need to leave it open. In fact, it is not about how open the door is, but rather how present the person inside that office is or isn't. Here is how a client, Andrew, at Ford Motor Company uses the 5 Gears:

In the past year, I moved into a new position with a team of 16 amazing people. It was important for me to maintain an open door policy to allow team members to talk through ideas, discuss issues, or just to catch up. The challenge was when I was working on something that required my focus and I was in "the zone" getting it done. That is when the open door policy created challenges, because not only did an interruption break my concentration, it created an unfair situation for my teammate. Since I was so focused on getting the work done, I had trouble giving them my undivided attention. Unintentionally, my open door policy was working against both of us.

That is when I introduced the 5 Gears to my team. We talked about what each gear meant and how we need to have a balanced approach to our lives leveraging all 5 gears. The team embraced the concept and we discussed how we could use the gears to introduce a common language through the organization.

Now, when I am [in] my "zone" and a teammate drops by, I hold out my hand and say, "I'm in 5th gear. Can it wait?" There are no hard feelings and we both know that it's not personal, just trying to get something done. If it is important, then I will stop and walk out of my office to refocus myself to serve their needs. If it can wait, then I will make a note and ensure I swing by once I get through the current project.

This new language allows us to communicate without any hard feelings when the time is not right to address something that is not critical. In addition, I found that other members of the team are using the language not only with me but they are beginning to use it with each other. Now, when someone is too busy to talk, there is not water cooler gossip that person X is not being a team player. Everyone knows that that was not a good time and they regroup when everyone is in 3rd or 4th gear.

Andrew's story is a prime example that demonstrates how our 5 Gears metaphor is a practical tool that works brilliantly in real life. This language was born out of the frustration of not being able to communicate with one another, our families, and our team members. What we have experienced (also known as our failures) has given rise to a language that, now, can be communicated using a symbol, a gesture, or a word that allows people to know where we are without judgment or confusion.

Stuck in 5th Gear

Along with success stories like Jeff's and Andrew's, there is also the inevitable flip side. Tales of Tom stuck in 5th gear all day and missing out on his kid's life, or the one where Susan looks at you with a blank stare when you ask her if she wants to go to lunch. 5th gear is helpful, but it can also be damaging. Certain personality types so love this gear that they begin to crave it, longing to escape into their own little world. The problem, though, is the disconnect that results from being in overdrive too much or for too long, Eventually, tensions arise for those relying on the 5th gear enthusiast—the team members who need their communication, or the boss awaiting a report, or even, yes, the wife and children waiting for Dad to finally come home.

People can actually get stuck in 5th gear and become quite cynical of the other gears or of people who tend to be in 2nd or 3rd. We have actually seen that introverts have a much easier time in 5th gear than extroverts. It makes sense as 5th gear can give introverts the time they need to think, process, and work. As for extroverts, 5th gear can feel like they have just gotten time out from their parents for something they did wrong.

Helping people get unstuck from 5th gear is crucial for communication and connectivity.

The key to understanding 5th gear is to understand what gear you are in and to then learn how to read the signs from others if you need to shift or get unstuck from the 5th gear you so love.

Missing Out

For those who remain stuck in 5th gear, they often do not realize or will not admit that they might just be missing out. 5th gear can create tunnel vision for people, causing them to miss opportunities to connect with others, learn something new, or simply encourage someone that is in their life.

A great example of this happened at an NBA basketball game in New York. If you have ever seen an NBA game, you will know that during commercial breaks, the events team will sometimes create a kiss cam where a cameraman finds a couple in the audience and the crowd cheers them on to give each other a kiss. Sometimes the camera crew will focus on an older couple or newlyweds, and then other times they will throw in the proverbial awkward shot of two people who may or may not want to kiss in front of 20,000 people.

A funny kiss cam incident occurred at a New York Knicks game at Madison Square Garden and was captured on video and posted on YouTube by eyewitness Hugo Davies, a British student in New York City. Observe how being stuck in 5th gear caused a guy to miss out on a great opportunity. Here are the details:

A quick-thinking woman who was snubbed by her date after being thrown live on a kiss cam scored an instant payback by passionately kissing the man seated next to her.

"I was filming the kiss cam as it was the first time I've ever been live to see one," Davies told *The Blaze*. "Most people went along with it and kissed their partner. However, this event suddenly happened and I was shocked that she did that as I thought she was the girlfriend of the first guy. So when she kissed the stranger, I was shocked," he continued. "The whole crowd went crazy."

In the video, the unidentified woman can be seen trying to get her date's attention to no avail. He was totally absorbed in the game. She then turns to the man seated beside her and the two lock lips, immediately grabbing the other guy's attention.

Davies told *The Blaze* that it all appeared "spontaneous," adding that the woman's date stood up "ready to confront the stranger" after it all went down. "His face was bright red for the rest of the game," Davies said.

Millions of people miss out on opportunities every day simply because they are stuck in 5th gear, or they were in the wrong gear at the wrong time, whether it was the missed kiss or the missed promotion or the missed chance to influence or encourage someone dear to you.

> Millions of people miss out on opportunities every day simply because they are stuck in 5th gear, or they were in the wrong gear at the wrong time.

Locking into 5th gear can produce good things with its hyper focus and productivity, and it can also create unhealthy habits and unknowing pain if not addressed. The secret is to know yourself so that you can begin leading yourself. Do you know what it is like to be on the other side of you?

Healthy and Unhealthy 5th Gear

Remember that 5th gear is the hyper-focus gear. It is meant for overdrive, when you need to get into the flow to finish a project, or write a book, or focus on a task thoroughly. The secret to understanding the 5 Gears is learning how to shift up and down into the appropriate gear to maximize your influence.

Listen to this story of a great father leading his son through the recognition that he was stuck. Dan Frey, a GiANT senior associate in Atlanta, describes it like this:

It is amazing to see how such a simple tool can have such a massive impact in the workplace. However, my favorite 5 Gears experience comes from the home.

I'm in the process of raising a future world changer. My son Sam is 16 years old, and to this day has never made a B in his life. He achieved his second-degree black belt in karate by the time he was 10 and has now moved into cross-country running at his high school. He is an avid Boy Scout and will be an Eagle Scout before he is 17. He placed fifth in the country in his Future Business Leaders of America competition and above everything, he is wired to care for people. He is truly an old soul.

A couple months ago I noticed Sam was under pressure in his world. While still keeping the same upbeat personality about him, he seemed very intense. As he sat down to breakfast before school one morning, I simply set the 5 Gears slide next to him. I had never taught the gears to him. I said, "Check this out. I'm going to run upstairs to change and when I come back down let me know what you think." Upon my return he looked me in the eye and said, "Dad, I'm stuck in 4th and 5th gear." He could not remember the last time he was in 1st as he had mastered being in 5th at his young age.

On the one hand, I wanted to praise him for being such a hard worker, but as a father, I was concerned that he was pushing too hard. Any man knows it's hard to show weakness, especially to your father. I do not believe he would have ever come to me and admitted he was struggling. In that instant, the gears had us connected. He needed to hear that it was okay and, in fact, necessary to take time to rest, recharge, and enjoy time with friends and family.

The 5 Gears tool immediately aligned me with my son in a way that may never have happened otherwise. It teed up a great lesson for Sam and let him know that I am in his corner. To this day, he uses the language of the gears when communicating at home.

Whether you are at home or at work, helping people get unstuck from 5th gear is crucial for communication and connectivity. We can help people become more socially aware and understand how to improve their emotional intelligence when we help them shift.

Teaching Others How to Use 5th Gear

You can actually train people to use 5th gear appropriately in a way that will take away the subjectivity. Here are a few examples for you to implement right away.

- If you are going to be in 5th gear for some period of time, send an email out to your team letting them know that at a certain time you are going to be in 5th gear, and if they need anything before or after just to let you know.
- Printing "5th Gear" on a sheet of paper and posting on your office or cubicle or door is a helpful way to communicate your need to focus (as long as it isn't always up).
- Simply holding up five fingers can communicate effectively, as well.

There are a number of ways to communicate 5th gear at work. Home is another frontier, especially if you have a home office. Listen to Tulsa businessman, Ryan Underwood, share how he has incorporated the 5 Gears with his young kids.

My daughters are 5 and 3. My wife and I work from home and the girls like to come and visit us in our office. We love it, and I keep a full stock of jellybeans on hand to await their visits. It is tough sometimes, especially if I am on an important call or videoconference because I never want the girls to think that I am not glad to see them. 5 Gears has helped us with this dilemma.

We taught the girls that if our office door is closed, they can knock, open it and whisper, "What gear are you in?" I've taught the girls the gears by simply holding up the number of fingers on my hand. They know that if I hold up a 3 or a 4 that it's okay to come in, hop on my lap, maybe even wave to those I'm conferencing with. BUT, if I hold up a 5, they are supposed to just blow kisses and close the door. "Daddy's in 5th gear and he'll come for me when he's shifted."

Those little rascals have realized the full effect of 5th gear means Daddy is unavailable. Not only am I not available for hugs; I'm also not available to stop them from getting into the jellybean jar.

However, if they knock and whisper, "Dad, what gear are you in?" And I flash a 5 . . . they always smile. Because the next thing they do is rush in like princess Special Forces in stealth mode and raid the jellybeans.

If a 3- and 5-year-old can learn the 5 Gears, then I am certain you can teach and train anyone in your work or your life how to shift gears or get in or out of 5th gear. When this occurs then people relax and get in to the right gear.

Getting 5th Gear into Your Life

Bob went to work every day and sat in front of a computer for eight hours. It was depressing. His mind wandered. At times he searched the Internet just to have some stimulation. When no one was around, he even watched television episodes on Hulu while he worked on his spreadsheets. He lived for the next "interruption" that would allow him to have human interaction. He was very capable of functioning well and getting the job done when people called or stopped by with needs. He was a gifted problem solver, but was in the wrong seat doing the wrong role.

After attending our Liberating Leader Tour event, he heard about the 5 Gears and realized that at this job he simply didn't have a fifth gear. He could readily function in 4th gear as long as the stimulation of new people and their concerns kept coming at him. But he simply didn't have the motivation to work alone on his computer hour after hour. Something had to change.

One of our GiANT senior associates took Bob through a Best Fit personality process to understand how he is wired. He discovered he was an extrovert stuck in an introvert role and began to understand that he is highly motivated and effective when interacting with people and when his work aligned with personal values. He thrived in an environment where creativity and innovation is appreciated. That was totally the opposite of his current work environment. Bob began to think back to times in his life when he had been productive and successful and easily entered into 5th gear. He realized that he was not defective or lacking as a person, but was simply a round peg in a square hole. In order to reinvigorate his work life, he needed a change—he needed to be in a situation where he could interact with people in an organization where the mission aligned with his personal values.

Long story short. . . . Bob is no longer in a cubicle with his computer. He found a great fit working in an HR department where his primary responsibilities include functions as a corporate trainer, giving the new employee orientation, and even apprenticing other employees so that they can find their paths to productivity. Bob found a position that complemented his gifts and passions. He has reclaimed his 5th gear, as for him it was a function of being in an extroverted role with people where he could see he was making a difference.

What about you? Have you lost your fifth gear? It might be as simple as being in the wrong role. For others, it might be that you have not created the boundaries that you need to close the door, communicate that you are in fifth gear, and become productive. You might even need to change locations in order to be more productive.

After thoroughly looking at 5th gear, whether you have lost it or whether you are consumed by it, take some time to observe these warning signs of an unhealthy 5th gear and what it looks like to have a healthy 5th gear.

Warning Signs: You know you have an unhealthy 5th if you . . .
- Allow personal health issues, exhaustion, or burnout to affect your life.
- Have long-term relational issues due to your work or hobby.
- Overuse 5th gear and tend to crash into an unhealthy 1st gear.
- Miss out on true life and the things that matter long term.

- Notice people around you hinting that you are working too much.
- Make it a pattern of eating meals in front of the computer or working instead of connecting.
- Stop being asked by people to be involved in social activities or casual connections.
- Have connections only with people you work with.

How Do You Get Healthy?
- It is important to master your settings, by starting to schedule 1st, 2nd, 3rd gear moments into your over-worked life.
- Let people know when you are going to be in 5th gear and put a time frame on it with accountability.
- Teach them the sign language so they can help you by knowing when it is time to shift to other gears.
- Think about what you want people in your life to say about you and adjust your actions accordingly.
- Schedule a vacation with those you love most and turn off all your electronics for at least 48 hours minimum.
- Use triggers and markers to help you shift to the appropriate gear and practice it daily.

Key Question—What do you think is causing you to overwork and how do you think it impacts those closest to you? Let someone you trust help you process this.

The 5th Gear Challenge

Plan your 5th gear for an entire month on your calendar and practice entering in and shifting out of it with diligence to see how much work you can get done as well as how well you can shift out of the gear.

The 5 Gears work as long as you make them work for you. Now that we understand how 5th gear works, let's spend some time understanding the gear that almost everyone experiences in the task-driven world in which we live, 4th gear.

5 ⚙

4th Gear— Leading in a Task World

Over the past two years we have shared the 5 Gears with thousands of people. Every time we share it we ask the leaders to tell us which gear they are normally in the most. Eighty-five percent of the time it is 4th gear. It's no wonder. We live in a task-driven, task-dominated world. To-do lists, task sheets, and productivity tools flood the market as adults are trying to get organized, stay organized, and become as proficient as possible in their world.

This desire for productivity from individuals, bosses, and organizations leads to a tendency to move from one task to the next, checking things off throughout the day without slowing down much, if at all. And so we move in a given day from phone calls to meetings to emails to meetings to calls to texts and maybe some project work before we head home. That is a normal day for the majority of people in the marketplace.

Add to this style of working the dizzying speed of technology, the frenetic pace of social media, and the unrealistic expectations of others to make things happen on a moment's notice and you have an exasperated, stressed-out workforce.

Waking Up in 4th Gear

Task-mindedness can become a habit or, rather, a way of life. People can become so married to their to-do lists that the daily tasks begin to control our lives—like a tail wagging a dog. I spoke with a general manager of a development company who stated that she doesn't know what life would look like without 4th gear. When she wakes up, she has a laundry list of emails awaiting her with tasks from others for the day ahead. The interesting thing is that she has done the same thing to others by trying to get one more email written before she goes to bed at night. These lists create drama, stress, and unceasing activity. She admitted that she was dominated by the tasks at hand that are often more urgent than important.

Sound familiar?

I'm going to ask you a question. But before I do, I want you to be completely honest with yourself. Do you normally check your email when you first wake up? Do you catch yourself just needing to "catch up on the day" really fast before getting in the shower or getting dressed? Do you know what you are doing to yourself? I ask only because this is a habit I suffer from at times as well.

From the moment our eyes open we have a choice. We can either wake up out of our sleeping recharge and warm up through a series of recharge exercises that could include reading or exercise or relational connection or we can look at email and let it set the tone of our day. If you start with email or your to-do list then you are letting tasks drive your priorities for the day. Some of you have extremely important jobs and a check-in is necessary to make sure the organization is fine after a night of sleep. I understand. However, when it becomes a pattern it truly can derail your true influence and mindset for the day.

4th gear is not a bad gear to be in. In fact, it's a great one to know how to use well, but there is a caveat: Just like the dangers of staying in 5th gear too long, we need to be careful how to use 4th, as well. Jumping directly to 4th gear is like trying to pull out of your garage in your car and shifting from reverse directly to 4th—it is virtually impossible.

Have you ever noticed how a sports team gets ready for a big game? Have you paid attention to what they do and do not do? Once they are dressed, they normally come out and stretch or practice shooting and do some warm-up drills. They do not rush from the locker room to the field and begin playing. Players need to warm up so they don't injure themselves, and so they can get their bodies and minds synchronized before the competition begins. And just like players need a warm-up, so do the rest of us—employees, leaders, families, students, humans in general. We need to start our days in the right gear and 4th gear is simply not it.

What 4th Gear Does to Our Brains and Our Work

If you have ever left work feeling tired and wired at the same time, it may not be the coffee or the late afternoon chocolate making you jittery. Instead, it may be the overconsumption of

4th gear. When we train our minds to multitask for long periods of time, we receive a garbled mix of data, people, and tasks. An example would be if we worked all day on our computers just opening files without closing any of them during the day. Our computer screens are full of information and consequently it is hard to find what you need in a moment because of the mess that has been made. That is life when we are consumed by 4th gear.

Dr. Jarrod Spencer, a renowned sports psychologist and friend, shares that our minds are like computers. At night our minds begin closing and sorting the files that we have opened all day into the proper locations or files. He goes on to share that those of us who are constantly opening up files without ever fully closing them at the end of the day normally have a harder time sleeping than others.

Sleep patterns, relationship dynamics, and overall peace of mind are just a few areas that are adversely affected when we stay stuck in 4th gear, consumed by our tasks. While technology has promised to help, it often only enables access for MORE: more tasks, more emails, more actions, more conversations, more information, and more stress.

Mark Herringshaw, one of our regional partners at GiANT Worldwide, shares some insight on this topic about one of our manufacturing clients. "The engineers I've met in this company live in 4th gear. Their days on the remanufacturing lines are filled with reaction action. A problem arises; they adapt. A message arrives; they respond. Forget an action list. Their agendas are improvised on the fly by others." This is an issue for many companies, as the tasks of one person, especially if they have a dominating personality, can become the priorities of many that day, deferring their own priorities until another day.

Mark goes on to share some of the growth that has taken place after implementing the 5 Gears. "We are learning how to do 4th gear more effectively. One of the best steps to improved productivity we've seen has been the simple injection of intentional 5th gear time. It's a necessary luxury that if they don't make happen, it never will. So, many are locking themselves away, perhaps for no more than an hour, three times a week. Some put signs up that say, 'Go away until 3:00.' Some leave the building to find time to get ahead to think."

In this case, 5th gear is the proper way to manage the overstimulation of 4th gear, especially in a highly stressful manufacturing, to-do culture. 5th gear is a natural shift when you have so much on your plate that needs to be focused on. By simply disciplining yourself and letting other people know you will be out for a period of time, you can knock a big project off your list, feel better about yourself and get back into your 4th gear routine.

The truth is that when we don't manage 4th gear well, it can take over our lives and begin to take us on a ride where we begin to lose our souls a bit. We wind up feeling like robots on an assembly line, or appearing that way to those around us. The tasks take over, our personality changes, and our work suffers a bit.

Mike Oppedahl, our managing partner at GiANT Worldwide and a phenomenal leader from Albuquerque, New Mexico, describes this perfectly here:

In my last organization, I had a mid-level director/leader in my organization named Shelley. Shelley is a rock star and like a cruise missile as it pertains to her work, and she has a very high capacity. In a staff meeting with our administrative team, we introduced the 5 Gears tool. There were many revelations throughout the team, but Shelley was speechless. Later that week, she requested a one-on-one meeting to discuss her leadership learning opportunity. She started off the meeting by stating that she had never had this kind of insight into her personal development in all her 20 years of leadership. Having been a high performer her entire career, Shelley had never needed to work on increasing her productivity by a significant magnitude. The 5 Gears helped her realize that she thought she was always in 5th gear, but in reality, she lived her leadership life in 4th gear, constantly being interrupted by her teams. As an extrovert, she had a tendency to want her door open during the entire working day and she had never learned what it was like to truly get to 5th gear and really focus on moving the needle. Because she was a high performer, she put tremendous pressure on herself to succeed at all costs. This led to a consistent 7 A.M. to 7 P.M. workday for her. After this incredible learning in her "self" circle of influence, Shelley began to spend intentional time in 5th gear every week. The immediate result was that she was able to achieve significantly more in her responsibilities and her team felt even more supported. The positive result in her "family" circle of influence was that she started leaving the office by 5:30 P.M. and was able to have dinner with her husband (who had become accustomed to eating alone).

Wow! Think about that. One subtle realization could possibly change the relational dynamics across the board. Now, imagine that being you. For the 85 percent reading this who are addicted to 4th gear, it is time to put it in the right order. Some of you simply need to shift gears to 5th and block the time out to truly get things done before shifting again into 3rd, 2nd, or 1st at the end of the day.

Remember, 4th gear is not bad. In fact, I encourage you to get as good as you can in that gear so that you are appropriately productive. However, I find it amazing that there are gurus who write and speak on maximizing 4th gear and yet don't understand that it is not as much about 4th gear as it is about knowing how to shift to the right gear at the right time.

The Different 4th Gears—Work and Home

Now, let's go deeper. 4th gear is not just for work. There is actually a 4th work gear and a 4th home gear, and while they look similar, they are different in the tasks and characters. Can you picture this? Waking up in 4th gear, being in 4th gear at work—all day—and then coming home only to switch to-do lists and maybe change clothes before continuing on with your to-do fetish?

Elizabeth Paul, a marketing guru, all-star leader, wife, and mom of three puts it this way:

> The personal story for me was realizing that as a woman I have "work" 4th and 5th gear and "domestic" 4th and 5th gear. I thought that because I was being disciplined about putting my devices away during the golden family window of 5 to 8 P.M. I wasn't in 4th or 5th gear, when in reality I was just putting on a different task hat. When my eyes were opened to that, I realized that I actually have little to no 3rd or 1st gear in my life at all. That was shocking.
>
> Like a lot of working moms, I put heroic effort into making sure that my work commitments don't adversely affect my kids/husband. I do this by getting up first, going to bed last, and sprinting like crazy any time they're in school,

napping, and so on, so they don't "feel" my working quite as much. Basically I completely sacrificed 1st gear in the service of 2nd (with husband/kids) and 4th/5th. Those gears felt like "have to haves" whereas 1st (any time for personal recharge) and 3rd (non-specific time) felt like luxuries that could go. Diagnostically seeing those holes made me realize why I've been feeling so tired and frayed. In order to make it all work, I've had to be ruthlessly efficient with my time—which has meant little time for non-"purposeful" or "happenstance" connecting points (3rd gear) and even less time to put fuel in my own tank (1st gear). Haven't exactly fixed that yet, but I hear admitting you have a problem is the first step toward recovery!

Elizabeth is spot on. Becoming aware of this leads her to an "aha" moment, which moves her to a breakthrough opportunity. When put into practice, this breakthrough could change the dynamics of her family forever and just might give her a renewed energy because she will be able to reprioritize her needed recharge and social time.

What It Is Like to Be on the Other Side of 4th Gear

A leader of an event business describes what it is like to lead a team in 4th gear. This example is a perfect way to process how to adjust and shift once you get to reality:

We are in the events business. Our logistics teams pretty much run in 4th gear through an entire event with a focus on getting things done, but also being available to help others who need it. Our training team, however, shifts in and out of

4th and 5th gear throughout an event. If they are training all day . . . they are likely in 5th gear. So, you have two sets of people . . . both working eight hours . . . but . . . they are in two different gears for most of the day. When our training team finishes, they are worn out and tired, while the logistics team is still ready for more.

Our logistics team, unknowingly, tends to judge the training team, thinking they are being lazy and don't want to do the grunt work when, in essence, they need recharge time. As their leader who can see the combination of personality styles as well as gear reality, I can now see what is really going on and what it is like to be on the other side of each group. Now we have language and the tools to analyze what's really going on and take preventive action.

We now plan ahead by scheduling downtime within the context of events so that everyone can recharge. Some need it . . . some don't. But, the key thing is that we're able to avoid perception issues. And the training team now knows when their recharge time is and doesn't have to try to "get out of something" in order to get the time they need to rest.

That is how a leader should lead. He knows himself to lead himself and knows the tendencies of his team. He understands the tendencies of his different groups and is proactively aligning them based on what gear they should be in, while eliminating the natural drama that occurs in most work settings.

Reprioritizing What Really Matters

Why do we let 4th gear control us? Is it the fear of possibly letting others down or is it a habit to allow tasks to run our lives? "Yes to both," some might say. We have choices to make and our hope is that this concept and the stories within it might cause us to reprioritize the little things so that the big things of life become more healthy and effective. When 4th gear controls us, we lose the ability to connect well and our presence with others tends to be limited at best.

This is one of my favorite stories. It is from a client/friend of ours in a large public company. She asked to remain nameless, but was thrilled to share the story. Notice how she became aware of her tendencies and chose to not be controlled by 4th gear in this important relationship:

My father is ill. The two things that he could do to improve his physical condition most significantly are to eat better and exercise. The two things he refuses to do are eat better and exercise. After our first GiANT Exec Core retreat in June 2014, I realized that I was spending all of my time with my father in 4th gear. I was reviewing medications, talking about diet, preparing food, setting up exercise routines, and contacting physical therapists. I had never really thought about it from my father's point of view. I asked myself what gear he might want me to be in during our time together. I knew 4th gear was not the answer. He certainly had expressed his irritation at my constant "nagging."

Since then, I have focused our time together being in 3rd gear, frequently shifting down to 2nd and occasionally up to 4th when there is an issue where he needs my help. (I certainly have not neglected any of his physical needs.) Over the last six months, he has lost significant weight and his health has continued to decline. If I had continued to nag at him from 4th gear, would he be in better physical condition? I don't know, but I suspect not. What I do know is that we have spent many precious hours together in 2nd gear.

We have discussed his faith on many occasions and his questions about grace and eternal life. He has shared many stories, memories, and life lessons with me. We've talked in-depth about his grandson Garrett's future. Dad told me many times that I might love Garrett *as much* as he did, but there was no way that anyone in the world loved him *more* than he did. Garrett feels the same way about his grand-dad. I know that he needed to talk to me so that he could see what the future looks like for his special buddy—his education, his career, his wife, his family. He has told me his hopes and dreams for Garrett and special things he'd like for him to experience. I know he knows I'll carry those forward for him. He is now confident that Garrett is going to be OK and told me he isn't worried about him anymore.

We have shared and connected on an intimate level as father and daughter. So while I was previously focused on the nourishment and health of my father's failing body, I changed focus to the nourishment and health of our relationship and his soul.

I've never told my father about the 5 Gears, I just showed him. I don't know if he has recognized that things are different or not. I do know that I am so glad that I was there to have these conversations with him. There is no one else he talks to the way he talks to me. In giving to him, I have received so very much in return.

My father won't be with me too much longer. I am so thankful that God used you to open my eyes before I was at a point of irreversible regret. I won't have to say, "If I had it to do all over again, I'd spend more time just being with my father and making sure he knew how much I loved him."

This is what a responsive leader looks like—someone who can lead themselves and adjust along the way to make a tough situation better.

Why Using All the Gears Makes 4th More Productive

4th gear is the work gear. It is the natural multitasking gear of which some of us are much better than others. And yet, if you will take the time to implement the other gears in your life you will find that your everyday, multitasking 4th gear will become more productive.

- You will finish projects while in 5th gear, which will make 4th gear feel more productive.
- When you insert 3rd gear appropriately (which is the next chapter) you will become much more at ease with people and will watch your influence climb because you are not too distracted by the cloud of tasks hanging over your head.
- If you insert 1st gear recharge into your task world you will have more energy and more peace about you.
- When 2nd gear is used correctly the people most important will become prioritized above the urgent tasks, which will lead to healthy relationships and, again, peace for you.

Practice getting better at 4th gear and learn to insert the other gears for your best and the best of those you lead and love. If you have a hard time getting into 4th gear then find someone who is brilliant at it and begin to mimic what you see.

Let's get really practical and begin to look at how 4th gear may be controlling you in an unhealthy way and how to get healthy at shifting into the task gear.

Warning Signs: You know you have an unhealthy 4th gear if . . .

- You consistently start your day with email.
- People notice you are obsessed by tasks.
- Achievement becomes the chief goal of your life.
- There are no boundaries on your time.
- Anxiety separation occurs when you are away from email or your phone.
- You are consistently drained and never fully charged.
- It takes a lot of effort to consistently get into a 2nd or 3rd gear context
- Struggling for consistent sleep is the norm and the mind is always racing.
- Your spouse, kids, and friends know that tasks come first.
- You are physically present, but intellectually and emotionally absent.
- There is a lot of activity but no real sign of progress.

How Do You Get Healthy?

- Replace email in the morning with something more inspirational—whatever helps you come alive.
- Be proactive, not reactive—don't let someone else define your day in an email or phone call.
- Discipline yourself by turning your phone off, or leaving it behind!
- Teach your family the 5 gears sign language so they can help you.
- Use boundaries, scheduling, trigger points, and markers to help you.

Key Question: Why do I allow others' tasks to run my life and dominate my agenda? Let someone you trust help you process this.

The 4th Gear Challenge

Replace email before breakfast with something that inspires you. Trade up to something that charges you for the day.

6 | ⚙

3rd Gear—Why Being Social Matters

Do you like coffee shops? How about going to a great dinner with a group of friends? That's what 3rd gear is all about, being social. Now some of you reading this will resound with a quick "Yes" to my initial question. Others of you are considering skipping to the next chapter. Please don't. If you are the type of person who gets stuck in 4th and 5th gear, I encourage you to give 3rd gear a chance. What you learn might just change the way you work or communicate.

Let's start with some examples of what 3rd gear actually looks like:

- Lunch with Colleagues—Conversations that are not dominated by work projects or tasks, but are a mix of humor, small talk, life, and a bit of work.

- Weekend Party—Time with friends or family around the pool, or a relaxed, casual barbeque with neighbors or friends.
- Round of Golf—Taking time with friends or clients to change the scenery and get to know each other better.
- After Work Gathering—Spending time with co-workers celebrating a birthday or special event.
- Game Night—Laughing, playing, and enjoying the company of a group of people, like your family or friends.
- Meal with Friends or Family—Breakfast, lunch, or dinner with a close group of buddies or friends.

3rd gear is a mindset. It is the space between task-driven, hyperfocused work and the no-work, relational connection of being with your family, spouse, or close friend. That in-between space can be onerous to manage. For some, work is comfortable. That is where your identity is and where you are confident in your competency. For others, work is tiring. Your identity lies in your social group, whether that's a club or a sports team or a special group of some sort.

Why Business Happens in 3rd Gear

Ever play company golf or take clients out to a special event or dinner? There is a reason why companies spend resources doing social events. It is where business really happens—in the relationship.

Gatherings like these represent 3rd gear time and it is vital to the success of the organization. Why? Because when you spend time with people outside of the normal 4th and 5th gear time you are focusing on the relationship—talking about family, history, sports, and the like. This time of relationship building allows those you are with to know you better and vice versa. They are observing

> *3rd gear is where business really happens—in the relationship.*

your character, going deeper than a one-hour meeting, and deciding whether or not they want to be around you for any length of time or do business together.

Business happens on the golf course. Not just transactional business, but long-term business. You get to know one another. The same happens at a social event or at a pub.

A different setting shows a different side of a person. I will never forget playing golf in Scottsdale with an executive from Walgreens. My initial thought of the guy was not bad or good. Frankly, I thought the guy was a bit stiff until he pulled out his driver and began to lose golf balls. He lost 28! He had to borrow eight from me, but in those 18 holes we knew more about each other, laughed our heads off, and began a relationship in business that was fun and easy. All because we both shifted into 3rd gear and took the time to understand each other.

Shifting into 3rd gear is not as hard as you might think. Here are some ways for you to get there. What are you interested in doing? What are your hobbies? Do you know anyone else who is interested in those same things? Could you gather some people together to talk about or do those things? That is where most connections happen.

Learn to Be Curious

Most of my career has been spent being curious when I meet people. I know that my personality drives me to do this, but whether you are hard-wired to be curious or not, I have discovered this is a valuable attribute to develop where 3rd gear is concerned, because it forces you to slow down. I leverage my curiosity by engaging the other person with questions about things that I naturally want to know more about. Here are some questions I frequently ask that help me connect with people and be present in 3rd gear space. You can try these out, too:

- "Where is your hometown?" This gives context. If I know someone from there we talk about that person.
- "Who is the most famous person from your town, or what is something unique about where you live?" This gives people the chance to brag about their town or a person and always brings a laugh or interesting conversation.
- "What do you love to do outside of your work?" You can get surprising answers to this question. One executive I asked responded back quickly with, "I like to sing, dance, and drink wine!" My quick response was, "You mean, all at once?" It led to a serious laugh and a conversation about stage productions and a whole new perspective on an area I knew nothing about.

To socially connect with others is to learn how to be present and to be curious about what they are interested in and what they like to do. If this is not a natural inclination of yours, try asking some of the questions above and see what happens when you let yourself spend some time in 3rd gear.

I will never forget the 3rd gear experience that happened after asking a leader from San Antonio about his passions and hobbies. He said, "I love professional wrestling!" I raised my eyebrows and thought, "Alright then." The funny part was that his answer was the last thing I thought he would have said. If he had stated, "I like to collect stamps," that would have matched up to my expectations based on what he wore and how he talked.

Fast-forward six hours. He managed to find an extra ticket for me to go with him to a big wrestling event that evening, and there I was, standing with him in an arena with thousands of wrestling-crazy fans, helping him hold a sign he made that said, "Everything is better Stone Cold," which was a reference to the WWF legend, Steve Austin.

We had a blast, and I laughed incessantly, cheering through the noise and the antics with my new friend. He invited me to experience something he really enjoyed, and it all started with me being curious and asking a simple question. What would I have missed if I never asked that question, if I had assumed he was a stamp collector?

On a side note, we happened to do business for years. My goal in that experience was not to be transactional, but instead to truly understand him and to get into his world. We had a great time and I added a new experience into my repertoire of 3rd gear activities.

To socially connect with others, learn to be interested before being interesting.

Ideas versus People, Places, or Things

3rd gear is the mode for being present in social places with a variety of different people. In studying this space we have noticed that there is a reason that some people have a hard time shifting into this social mode.

My good friend Renzi Stone, CEO of Saxum Communications in Oklahoma City, shared a conversation he had been having with his friend, Kate Richards, CEO of Warwick Energy. Kate has homes in New York City and Oklahoma City and shared an observation that has been a big a-ha for me: people in larger cities tend to talk about and discuss ideas, whereas people in smaller towns often talk about people, places, or things.

This made so much sense to me, as I was transitioning from London to Oklahoma City, back to my home state. After living in large cities like Atlanta and London, I realized I needed to make sure that I had a group of friends around me that liked to talk about big ideas, in order to dream big. (You will remember my saying earlier in this book that I know this about myself. Big ideas are a big deal to me.) I tend to thrive in 3rd gear settings that are full of people talking about big ideas. Conversely, I tend to put up with conversations about their grandkids, their vacations, or their cars.

This is not an urban versus rural conversation, but a reality that there are certain people in big and small cities who like to talk about ideas and other groups of people that like to talk people, places, and things. That is not bad, it just is.

Therefore, some of you have a hard time entering into conversations with people who are consumed by their ideas and are not interested in your family or job, while others of you are dying in conversations filled with the vacations that others are hoping to experience.

As I was having a conversation with Renzi, he went on to share this: "Our lack of being present is often about us tuning others out because what they are saying isn't interesting, which in itself is filled with pride and arrogance. We rarely tune out interesting conversation. We normally listen to things that are compelling. The key is being respectful even when we couldn't care less and the content is less than interesting."

I love the point he is making, that being present requires the heavy lifting of listening to the talks about the weather or sports or travel to get to something more substantial, to relational gold.

Since that conversation I have entered every 3rd gear setting analyzing which type it will be and asking myself: Will the folks here want to talk about ideas or people/things? When I figure out the direction, I work hard to be as curious as I can, focused on honoring the other person and giving them the respect they deserve. It is amazing to watch how the other person begins to come alive and how I, too, become present in that moment.

How 3rd Gear Can Increase Your Influence

When you do 3rd gear well you will notice your influence increase dramatically over time. It is partly due to the respect that others give you because you respect them, but it is also due to the demeanor and confidence that naturally occurs inside you. People are attracted to confident people, and there is a direct correlation between confidence and respectful curiosity.

Why? It shows that you know how to converse with people and are humble enough to listen to others successes without feeling jealous. Doing 3rd gear well endears people to you. This respect leads to increased influence, which leads to more opportunities. This is why I wrote *Making Your Leadership Come Alive,* to help leaders understand that leadership is influence and influence is power. When our intent is pure we will use the power to empower,

Social mode is worth it. Do it right and watch your influence climb.

not overpower. Thus, doing 3rd gear well leads to encouraging others and garnering the respect of others.

Let's try to break this down even more logically so you can see for yourself how 3rd gear can increase your influence. Imagine yourself at a more formal social gathering with colleagues and friends.

1. You sit at a table making casual conversation.
2. You then begin to small-talk about things like the weather or the weekend game.
3. This normally leads to honing in on a conversation with one or two people closest to you.
4. You listen, chime in and add value, or you listen and move on to the next conversation. Some of the conversation might go into 4th gear, where people begin talking about work or a project, ideally with a shift back into 3rd gear. Some people want to stay in 4th, while others naturally moved back into 3rd.
5. Over the course of an hour you have learned a lot about people. Some of them you like and want to learn more about, while with others you vow that was the last time you want to be around them.
6. At the end of the night you revisit your time and decide that you want to get to know a few people better, to which you set up a time and get together with them at a future date.
7. Your 3rd gear conversation led to possible 2nd gear connections with people you want to get to know better or 4th gear opportunities if you met someone that you could help or could help you in your work.

This pattern happens all the time. I was talking to a respected leader recently who shared her experience about attending a social gathering of new acquaintances. She described what happened as the 20 ladies she was with milled around trying to get to know each other. It sounded amusing actually. Some retreated to the corner looking for one other like-minded soul to get to know. She, on the other hand, decided to go for it. She was an introvert who decided to mix and mingle with the best of them before finding the one person to connect into 2nd gear with.

Because this person is secure and confident, she could move in and out of conversations with little fear of being misinterpreted. In the end, she left feeling good about herself, knowing that she shifted appropriately into 3rd gear and walked away with a few people that she wants to get to know better. When asked if she wants to go back, she responded positively.

Because she engaged fully in 3rd gear, she established herself as a person whom others wanted to get to know as well.

What Happens When You Avoid 3rd Gear

Avoidance is a tactic of those who are either insecure and don't know how to communicate or arrogant and believe they are too important for "small talk."

If you allow your insecurities to grab hold of you and you shrink back into your comfortable place, you miss the opportunity to know others and be known. This is a fundamental sin of good leadership and it affects you more than you know.

Conversely, if in your busyness you treat people as if they are not as important as your work, then you lose respect over time and gain a reputation for being unapproachable.

Some of you might say, "But I am just not comfortable with groups of people."

I understand that it might be hard for you to connect. It may be that you have been hurt in the past or have an extremely introverted personality. Some of that might require some counseling or deeper conversation with someone you trust.

What is important, though, is in retreating to your comfortable space you might actually make it harder for yourself, not easier. When this happens you are actually losing influence: people not wanting to know you or connect with you. In time, it is like you have painted yourself in a corner.

When you learn how to do 3rd gear well, you open the door to fulfilling relationships and an improved reputation. Sometimes you have to trick yourself by making it a game to meet three people or get to know one out of twenty people. I am an extrovert and I have to do that at times as well, especially when I am tired. Yet, I know that when I connect, everyone wins. Learn to get comfortable in the social mode of 3rd gear and you will win more than lose, every time.

For Those Still Stuck in 4th and 5th Gear

Have we convinced you yet that 3rd gear is vital? Do you understand that when people feel that they are known then they actually begin to respect you? Do you see that when you don't engage at all then you get what you gave?

Most of the people I know who are stuck in 4th and 5th gear are simply busy people. They are busy doing and they usually are pretty good at what they do. If this is you and you want to get better at 3rd gear then let me leave you with some compelling action steps:

1. Learn to be "for" people. People can sense if you are for them, against them, or for yourself. One way to get to 3rd

gear is to simply engage with them. Show that you are interested in them to some level.

2. If you are an idea person trapped in a 3rd gear setting with "people and things" people or vice versa, try your best to be curious. Develop discipline here. Move around if you need to, but at least show your interest.

3. Give people the opportunity to surprise you. You never know where this might lead, but someone could surprise you with a fact or an idea that might blow you away. Judging people before you meet is a recipe for boredom and snobbery.

4. Get off your phone. Put your phone away so that you are not tempted to pull it out and get into 4th or 5th gear. Like the kiss cam incident shared earlier in the book, you may simply miss out and never know it.

Whatever your area of growth, give 3rd gear a chance as you increase your influence on others. Engage. Listen. Learn. Be curious. Be present. You will be glad you did and you will see the opportunities for deeper connections happen more readily.

How to Help Others Get into 3rd Gear

Getting into 3rd gear is hard enough as it is. However, you can also help others get into social mode by using sign language. Let me give you an example. Raise your right hand. Hold up five fingers and take away two. That leaves you with the perfect symbol to help people shift into social mode.

A story to explain this comes to mind when Jeff and Donilyn Hodge decided to throw a social dinner for friends in Atlanta on our behalf. Donilyn Hodge knows how to throw a party! She had appetizers and drinks, entrees and party favors—classic Southern hospitality.

As the night went on, one of our associates walked in the house fresh from the airport. When he saw me he came straight to me sharing some successes he had had in referring some new prospective clients into our Executive Core. As he rattled off this and that in a flurry of excitement and 4th gear business, I looked at him and simply held my hand out showing three fingers.

He briskly stopped, smiled, and shifted. He turned immediately to his right and started connecting with the guy next to him, saying "Hi, how are you? Good to meet you!"

It was awesome. All I had to do was show three fingers. No drama or long conversation needed. Our associate got it. He shifted well into 3rd gear.

I could have said, "You know I so appreciate your enthusiasm and love your passion, but would you mind if we waited and talked about this at a better time?" Instead, I held up three fingers and he shifted.

All you need to do is help people shift. Teach the concept and metaphor. Use the sign language of 5 Gears consistently and watch it work.

Overdoing 3rd Gear

3rd gear can be just as dangerous as 4th and 5th gear if abused, especially if a person is insecure and is trying to get their identity from the social space.

I have watched one particular leader work so hard to connect to people in certain cities that when he arrives, he double- and triple- books his social calendar to be with people that he wants to connect with. The problem is that he becomes disconnected because his social schedule dominates his time with the actual people he wants to connect with.

In 3rd gear you can't control the moments of impact or the laughter or fun. When you try to control social space it actually becomes a 4th gear activity. In one instance this leader had booked two events back to back. He left five minutes before he was honored in a crowd of 40 people and never got to hear what others thought about him because he was fitting too many people into his 4th gear social planning.

To be present means that at times you have to go with the flow of the social setting so that you don't miss the inside jokes or the laughs or moments of 2nd gear connectivity.

Warning Signs: You know you have an unhealthy 3rd gear if you . . .
- Procrastinate and miss doing real 4th gear work.
- Need a party at all times.
- Have a lack of discipline and professionalism.
- Never go deep enough and remain superficial.
- Double-book relationships and miss the depth.
- Your colleagues think you're lazy or that work is a minor inconvenience.
- Feel like you have a mask, you never want to go deeper.
- Try so hard not to miss out that you actually miss out.

How Do You Get Healthy?
- Schedule time alone, recharge time, to learn to be all right on your own.
- Practice 5th gear time and put it in your schedule.
- Utilize discretion and discipline in how you communicate.

- Practice 2nd gear conversations in a 3rd gear environment.
- Commit to deepening at least one key friendship in your life.

Key Question: What's keeping you from working hard and going deeper with people? Process with someone in your life.

The 3rd Gear Challenge

Choose 3 relationships in your life that you want to deepen and create a plan for doing this.

Social mode is worth it. Do it right and watch your influence climb. Avoid it and you will miss more than you can imagine.

7 | ⚙

2nd Gear—
Connecting
Deeply

When was the last time that you truly connected with someone in a meaningful way? How did that experience make you feel? When was the last time you went deep with someone and left the meeting fully recharged?

This is what 2nd gear is truly about—the ability to shift into connect mode and become present with someone in your life who brings you joy. Whether work colleagues, family, or friends, it is time geared toward relationship building without an agenda or pressure to be productive.

We asked the leaders we work with in organizations of all shapes and sizes to describe what 2nd gear looks like, and here is their list:

- "Spending time with my son. Doing things that he and I love to do."
- "Going to lunch with a co-worker who understands me and allows me to vent."
- "Being with our kids and playing games without cell phones or TV."
- "Taking my wife out on a date. Spending time just being together."
- "Stopping by my employee's desk and checking in—spending more time than I normally would."
- "Being with my father, who is sick, and not nagging, but instead connecting."
- "Making a fire pit and trading funny stories with my family."
- "Getting quality time with my key leaders. Listening and then challenging them as they become better leaders."

What are your 2nd gear opportunities? Take some time to write them down. Now, make a list of all the people in your life and the moments where 2nd gear could take place. Are you spending purposeful time here, or are you skipping it?

It takes some practice getting into 2nd gear for some. Remember, you can use the sign language we talked about last chapter in your home or when appropriate. Hold up two fingers when the kids are on their phones at dinner. Or when your spouse is working on her laptop when it's time to watch your favorite TV show together. Life, work, tasks, people, and even our own multitasking minds can keep us shallow, distracted, and unable to really get to the levels of connection that allow our personal relationships to thrive.

Why Is It So Hard to Get to 2nd Gear?

You heard my opening story of being disconnected from my wife and kids. What is your story? How many of you have a hard time shifting out of task mode or focus mode? How hard is it to put your phone down and become present with the people around you? No matter what your role is, be it CEO, executive, entrepreneur, dad, mom, or employee, we all struggle to shift into 2nd gear.

One father I talked to shared how he gets easily distracted when coming home at night. He said, "I get frustrated with myself because I'm always pulled into the news or the weather or an app or an iPad game of solitaire." He went on to share, "I am always doing something or looking online and I know that my kids have stopped reaching out knowing I am not available. I know it, but I don't know how to get out of it."

This guy got real with me, sharing his concerns, and you could feel the tension mounting as he described his reality. He went on to share with me how he feels like he is losing his children, but cannot seem to figure out how to not be pulled into time-wasting entertainment. This man knows what he is doing is frivolous, but doesn't know how to start connecting. In situations like these, we have to get back to basics, and awareness of the problem is the first step toward breaking old habits.

Learning to Connect

It has to start somewhere. In the same way that there is a logical flow into 3rd gear, there is a clear path to connect via 2nd gear as well. Here are some tips to incorporate into your life and leadership.

1. **Take the time.** When you sense that there is an opportunity to connect, go for it. Make time to connect. Add connect time to your calendar or space your appointments out to add an extra 15 minutes or so, if and when you have a meeting.

2. **Listen.** The way to connect comes through your ears, not your mouth. When you listen, you give respect and gain perspective. Listening to others by hearing what is really going on is the start to connecting well and being present.

3. **Don't force it.** People know if you are forcing something. You can't fake connection. It is a two-way street. Inauthenticity leads to disconnection. Be you, be present, and be patient. Connection will happen if you will be present.

4. **Give yourself away.** Giving yourself away seems risky to some, especially to those who have been burned. However, when you risk by going deep and giving yourself away to help the other person, you increase your chances to receive far more than you imagined. When you invest well you normally get a return on that investment.

5. **Cut what binds.** This is easier said than done, but you may have habits in your life that are keeping you from your best or from key relationships. Surely solitaire or apps or TV can be prioritized for better times. Consider moving things to a different time of the day if they are having an adverse effect on your relationships.

What Happens When Everyone Is in 2nd Gear?

When people get in 2nd gear, everyone benefits. One of our senior associates from Phoenix, Debbie Correa, shared what happened to her when her family shifted together into 2nd gear:

My first experience with 5 Gears was when Jeremie shared this simple, yet impactful tool with a group of leaders on the back porch of a friend's house in Atlanta. That day I walked away with a newfound vocabulary for some very common issues with my family and business relationships. I became consciously aware of what it meant to be in 2nd gear and how I wasn't there often. As a realtor I have no set business hours. I work at any time of the day or night. As a result, I find that I can be texting or sending an email while cooking dinner or helping my kids with homework. This often frustrated my kids and they have often told me that I am constantly on my phone and not very present. I used to tell them that it was my job . . . that I wasn't texting friends about what to wear tomorrow but I was actually working so that they could live in a nice home. How is that for a layer of guilt?

My husband and kids are just as guilty. My husband works in IT and tends to wake up in 4th gear with his emails and go to bed finishing the next day's batch of emails. The kids, who are teenagers, seem to live on their phones, always checking for text messages from friends or online with social media. We all went around in circles being frustrated with each other because of the addiction to our phones that we all shared.

5 Gears is changing how we communicate as a family. We are all becoming consciously aware of our setting and our environment and we are working to apply the appropriate gear and the right time. We now have a common language that everybody relates to and appreciates to help us communicate better. I don't have to add any snarky

remarks, or guilt to express my feelings. All I have to say is "2nd gear" and I can get their attention and we all can adjust accordingly. It's absolutely wonderful!

5 Gears is a simple yet powerful tool. It has made a huge difference in my family and in me. It began at home and now I take it with me where ever I go. My work is getting better as well. By realizing my gear order and my natural tendencies I am now becoming the engaged mother and wife I want to be and I am also becoming consciously aware of my surroundings while socializing with friends or in meetings with clients. It is all about knowing who you are in order to lead yourself.

Debbie's story could easily be yours. The speed of our society and its social norms can easily cause frustration and disconnection with our family and friends. 2nd gear leads people to get engaged, to be present. It can work in any circle, from home to team to company to community. When everyone engages, everyone wins. That is the secret.

Truly Being Present

Who do you want to connect with? Are you being intentional to do that? Have you created space in order to connect well with those in your life?

Being present has been so difficult for me even as I write this book. We have a short deadline and I have noticed that I am writing almost around the clock. My family and I have discussed the fact that we are writing two books in one year and that it will take a lot of time, energy, and mental thought. And still, it is my responsibility to be the leader worth following in my home. Even with the pressure of a deadline, I still have to practice shifting.

My youngest daughter, Kate, asked me one evening if I wanted to play a game with her. My response is a bit embarrassing, but it makes the point. I told her, "I am sorry, sweetie, but I have to finish the chapter on 3rd gear." I actually said that. It took about 10 minutes for the full conviction to set in as I realized what I had said to her. I stopped writing, saved my work, and left to connect with her casually as much as I could. Interestingly, I had missed the window as she had joined in on a project with Mom. On one hand, I thought, "Okay, I can get back to writing," when in reality I had missed an opportunity to be present with her.

Is it sinking in yet? Being present in 2nd gear leads to:

- Healthy relationships that bring peace to your mind and heart.
- Fruitful growth between people.
- Better conversations and more inspiration.
- Likeability and trust.
- Reestablished priorities.
- Less drama and more security.
- Social awareness and emotional intelligence.

Another one of our senior associates, Tom Nebel, shared an example of this at one of our boot camps:

The understanding of 2nd gear has totally revolutionized how my adult son, Andrew, and I relate to each other. We regularly get together for "our time" (watching a movie or a game, or just having dinner), but his connectedness with others was getting in our way. His smartphone was always buzzing with text messages and other incoming data, and he'd engage with it. Mine would do the same on occasion, and I'd play along. We were frustrating each other because it was violating our space and the intent of being together, and we'd act out our frustration with aggressive and passive-aggressive behavior.

It was supposed to be "our time," but it would often bring out our worst because we didn't have the vocabulary and language to define what was happening. Then I pulled out the 5 Gears tool, and we talked it through. Right then and there we made a commitment that when we came together in this way we'd commit to being in 2nd gear.

Since then, when we get together, we acknowledge the gear, and we shut off the phones. It reminds me of the old western movies, when the cowboys would take their guns off at the saloon and put them in the middle of the table. There will be no aggression here—only camaraderie. It's been a remarkable change in how we relate, and we won't have it any other way.

This is a great example of intentional communication and real conversation. Imagine this happening with you.

- Imagine your family putting their technology on a side table and engaging for more than an hour together.
- Imagine being in a meeting with your boss where he or she isn't checking every buzz that occurs on their phone.
- Imagine locking eyes with someone and having a deep conversation that brings life to both of you.
- Imagine learning how to be naturally and authentically present with the people you are around on a regular basis.

When you are truly present you are giving yourself to another person for a period of time. You are giving your best for their best. 2nd gear is like giving a present to someone—a gift designed specifically for him or her, which you also get to enjoy.

> *2nd gear leads people to get engaged, to be present.*

Conversely, by not being present you are actually wasting their time. If a person comes to you fully present with an expectation to connect, then you have a choice to either downshift to 2nd gear or let them know that you are in 5th and schedule a time to allow you to downshift into the same gear at the same time. If you don't share, but stay distracted, then you are simply wasting the other person's time.

Kevin Deshazo, CEO of Fieldhouse Media, realized what he was doing in his relationship with his son:

5 Gears has been one of the more powerful tools for me that GiANT has introduced, both on a personal and family level. One specific story is with my oldest son, Gabe. When I'm not traveling, I take him to school in the morning and pick him up in the afternoon. While in transit I normally check my phone at red lights for emails and tweets, trying to see what the world is up to.

The 5 Gears mindset opened my eyes to realizing that this was crucial 2nd gear time with my son. This was our five to eight minutes each trip to connect as father and son and I was missing out on that opportunity. Everything changed.

Now when we get in the car I plug in my phone and turn on some music. On the way to school we talk about the day ahead and what he's excited about and I take a few minutes to encourage him and simply connect. On the way home we debrief about his day and what he learned that day. He knows he has my full attention. It is brilliant.

There's a noticeable difference in his mood, based on whether I'm in 4th gear, on my phone, versus being in 2nd gear, engaging him in conversation. I needed to meet him in the right gear. Now, I don't feel like I am missing the time that I know is short and he is getting the best of me.

Back to the Real World

2nd gear can be a reality. I know hundreds of leaders who have implemented 2nd gear firmly in their lives and redeemed the relationships they had singed through the years. On one occasion I was speaking to a leaders conference in Asheville, North Carolina. After sharing the 5 Gears, a guy came up to me with tears in his eyes. He could barely get the words out when he said, "It may be too late, but I am going to give it a try." He went on to share that his wife had left him the week before and that he had come to realize that it was he and his addictions to work, tasks, and the things that made him feel better that drove her away. He realized that everyone else got his best and his wife got his leftovers.

The real world should be each of us learning how to be real with each other and appropriately present for the benefit of each other. Hear again how Tom Nebel describes the way it should be. I love this:

Years ago my family took a vacation to Hawaii, and it was everything we'd hoped for. When the trip was coming to a close and we were at the Honolulu airport waiting to board the airplane, I was overhearing conversations from other tourists who were headed home as well. Again and again I would hear people say with resignation, "Well, now back to the real world." I understand. It's hard to say goodbye to a vacation.

But I thought about that, and something [was] triggered in me. I said to my family, "You know, I don't think we're headed back to the real world. I think we're leaving the real world. Our time together here was the closest thing to reality we've had in a long, long while. It's given us space to be as real as we can be. Let's start thinking about our getaways as the real world." Right then and there we planned our next vacation, and we made a commitment to never concluding a vacation without planning for the next.

The real world is each of us taking the time to connect, apprentice, and pass on what we have to others. The real world is about being consistent, not inconsistent. It is about giving our best to help others, not flitting around from one meeting to the next. Being present is the best real world and when it happens, you know it is true.

By the way, we are not suggesting that you change your life so you start going around hugging people and living in coffee shops, talking all day, like you see some people doing. Each gear has the appropriate time and place, just like a car uses all gears in different settings.

What we are suggesting is that most adults get so over-whelmed by work and the habits of being in 4th and 5th gear that they have a hard time learning to shift into 1st, 2nd, or 3rd. That is primarily why we are using stories and metaphors to bring you to your own reality. We hope that you will begin looking at your 4th gear life and possibly make the changes

Connecting is an art form. And it takes practice.

necessary to learn how to shift appropriately into the right gear for the benefit of you and everyone you are with.

By the way, when you are in 2nd gear correctly, it can fuel you up in your mind and emotions far more than you can by staying in 4th gear for that extra hour. It is amazing what happens psychologically and emotionally when you are at peace with those closest to you. You work smarter and produce more results when you are at peace with those in your life.

2nd Gear in a 4th Gear Culture

2nd gear is not very popular in our culture. While TV ads show families having picnics, experiences, or fun adventures together, the reality of our culture is directly opposed to the concept. Americans get two weeks a year for vacations. Workers show up early and stay late to please certain bosses, not because they are more productive, but because that is the culture their boss values. This is the "get it done" mentality and most of us experience this every day.

I have worked in cultures that push for productivity to such a degree that people are on edge constantly. The resulting lack of connectivity and relationships in these instances produces drama that causes divisions inside teams and organizations. Here you find much pain and very little gain. Conversely, I have been part of organizations where the people fight for the highest possible good of each other. They spend more time being connected and understanding each other, which corresponds directly to growth because of team alignment.

One of the things I value about the British culture is their ability to both work hard and to connect appropriately. Our British friends Andrew and Jess Jackson are great examples. He is a physician and she teaches French and Spanish in Beaconsfield, England. He would work hard, shift into 1st gear for personal recharge by taking a bike ride, and then end up at our home, Hedsor Priory, for a dinner over a bottle of wine for a 2nd or 3rd gear moment. There would be times that all of us would sit outside for hours enjoying a sunset and connecting deeply.

Long walks, rambles through the woods, and great conversations happened with most of our British friends. It happened all the time in the United Kingdom. 2nd and 3rd gears are much more culturally fitting in the United Kingdom than in the United States, in our opinion. Thus, the depths of relationships can often go much deeper in that culture than in parts of the task-driven U.S. culture.

This is not an indictment as much as it is an observation. Life is easier in the United States and the people are a bit nicer in the beginning. And yet, the performance culture and the task-driven lifestyles of professionals and parents can make the American culture friendly and shallow, whereas our experience living in London taught us that while Brits may be more standoffish at the beginning, they can connect more deeply at times.

Please don't misunderstand; we love 4th gear and the productivity of work. However, we have also experienced 2nd and 3rd gears and have seen the joys and benefits of knowing people deeply and developing business and work that is equally uplifting. It is not a battle between this and that, but rather a need for both 4th and 2nd gears.

Remember, connecting is an art and science. Practice connecting. Learn to shift into 2nd gear for the sake of each other. When you begin to master 2nd gear, you will begin to experience a deeper level of respect and trust.

Warning Signs: You know you have an unhealthy 2nd gear if . . .

- You obsess about the key relationships in your life and not the person you are talking to.
- The desire to go deep in conversation keeps you from 3rd gear connectivity.
- Talking too much and too long is your normal pattern.
- There is an inappropriate amount of time spent caring at work rather than working.
- You put unrealistic expectations on people to connect, make people feel bad, and eventually isolate yourself.
- You constantly struggle with having the right conversation in the wrong context.
- You are so present-focused, you struggle to see the big picture.

How Do You Get Healthy?

- Learn to have a 3rd gear social conversation and be okay with it.
- Discipline and discretion—know when it is the right time to have that conversation.
- Be careful to not put pressure on people to go deep when they are not ready.
- Be interested before trying to be interesting.
- Learn how to ask 3rd gear questions.
- Monitor how much time you spend in 2nd gear at work.
- Remember to be relevant in your connectivity: Does the conversation agenda relate to the person you are talking to?

Key Question: How might my desire to go deeper actually push people away?

The 2nd Gear Challenge

Commit to a particular area of study and professional advancement to get stronger in your 4th and 5th gear.

8

1st Gear— Learning to Recharge

How well do you rest? Do you take the time necessary to fully recharge?

Do you have an intentional recharge zone or a routine you have disciplined yourself to follow that helps you downshift to rest, refuel, and renew your energy?

When you are not recharged or fully rested, it is almost impossible to be present with someone else, let alone add value to his or her life. When you are charged up and rested well, then you have the ability to impact those around you, which will simultaneously impact your influence.

People in general do not know how to rest or recharge. Therefore they are less effective than they could be. The majority of people I know fall into this category of not knowing how to recharge. They might read an article on rest and say, "I need to do more of that." They believe they need to recharge and often talk about how worn out they are from all their hard work. And yet, when I ask them what they do to get recharged they say, "I'm just working through it. I will be okay, I'm just tired right now." Translated, this means, "I don't really know how to recharge and I want you to know that I am a hard worker, and feel bad for me and maybe encourage me a bit."

I can spot this behavior because I have lived it myself. In fact, 1st gear is not a gear I'm naturally wired to do well. But what I have discovered from my own failures is that if you fix your charging issues, if you figure out what 1st gear feels like for you and discipline yourself to spend time there, more power will flow through you. If you live and lead out of 20 percent battery life then you will never experience what you hope to experience.

It is three o'clock in the afternoon, and you hear the ding of your cell phone. It notifies you that you have 20 percent of battery life left. You are an hour away from an important phone call and you have no charger. Isn't that the way it is? You have an important event and no power left to complete it. We know we cannot, by sheer force of will, make our cell phones work when the batteries are dead. Why, then, do we think we can force ourselves to run well on empty?

> When you are charged up and rested well, then you have the ability to impact those around you, which will simultaneously impact your influence.

Spending intentional time in 1st gear is the key to recharging. It is the gear needed at the start of the day and the end of the day. Consider our car analogy: when we drive, we start in 1st, not 4th. Imagine what happens if you try to shift directly to 4th from neutral: The engine will stall, right? There is a natural progression to life and leadership in the same way. Starting in 1st helps you get into the day in a way that will not wreck your own internal transmission.

How We Recharge: Battery Pack or Solar Panel

Recharging does not happen the same way for everyone, though, and it is important to note that your natural personality and wiring will influence how you need to recharge. Steve Cockram is the master at explaining how to recharge. He states that "introverts recharge internally, like a battery pack. They need to plug into an energy source directly and recharge on their own from within. Extroverts, on the other hand, are like solar panels: their recharge happens from external power sources, like ideas or people or experiences."

Steve goes on to share some examples of typical battery pack–type recharge sources for introverts:

- Sleeping—introverts usually need a bit more sleep than extroverts
- Reading—like novels or biographies
- Exercise—long runs or walks alone
- Devotions—introverts are normally more disciplined with their personal time
- Meditation—this normally becomes a place for peace
- Time to yourself to pursue individual hobbies, like art, gardening, cooking, woodworking, and so on

And here are some typical solar powered–type recharges for extroverts:

- Time with a mentor—extroverts need to talk out loud to hear their ideas with someone they trust
- Ideas—some extroverts are enamored with ideas, which can bring life to them
- 2nd gear time—extroverts tend to get recharged with people, especially those they care for a great deal
- Enlivened experiences—a concert or movie can be recharging to an extrovert
- Sleep—extroverts need sleep as well, usually less than introverts
- Speaking—some extroverts thrive when they speak or share
- Reading—books that bring inspiration and are highly applicable
- Exercise—extroverts tend to like class-type exercise with a group of people rather than the isolated experience of running by themselves

Each of you could add others to the list, but this at least gets us started. And the method of recharge is not the issue; making sure you know how *you* need to recharge is. Do you know how you recharge? Or are you like most people and have simply gone along with the crowd, doing what everyone in your family or in society tells you that you should do? We will dive deeper in the next section to find out what works for you.

> *When you are not recharged . . . it's almost impossible to be present with someone else.*

What Recharge Looks Like for You

Everyone is different. We are a mix of introverts and extro-verts, pioneers and nurturers, thinkers and feelers, and so on. Like thumbprints, we are all unique in our personality hard wiring, and that means that we all recharge differently. The problem is that most of the articles on rest or recharging are generic, and when people try to apply the one-size-fits-all idea, there's no improvement. Here's how this plays out for Steve and me at home with our families:

Steve and I are extreme extroverts, while our wives are introverts, and our kids are a mix of both. We all recharge differently. Extroverts do not need as much time to themselves nor as much sleep, generally, as introverts do. Pioneers will spend hours with other idea creators who inspire them while nurturers will spend time with people they feel need their care. We are each wonderfully made and unique in our wiring, but you can well imagine the challenges and complications that arise in our own homes with all of us needing to recharge in different ways.

Knowing yourself well, and knowing those around you, then, is vital for effective recharging to take place. When you know yourself and what you need, then you can begin to lead yourself well, and the outcome is better connectivity in your relationships.

So what should 1st gear recharging look like for you? Here are some practical questions to help you know yourself better:

1. Are you an introvert or an extrovert?
2. How much sleep do you need? Do you get that amount regularly?

3. What prevents you from getting enough sleep?
4. How far do you drive to work (if you do)?
5. How busy is your morning time?
6. Do you have young kids?
7. If you are an introvert, do you take any time in the middle of the day to recharge?
8. What does your drive home look like (if you have one)?
9. What do you do in the evening?
10. What is your normal bedtime routine?
11. Are you a disciplined person by nature?

To know yourself is to lead yourself. Can you begin to lead yourself to recharging and rest? Can you begin to create your own profile to know how you rest and recharge?

For instance, I (Jeremie) know that as an extrovert I need about six hours of sleep at night. Because I am in a season of writing, speaking, and connecting with our clients in the United States, I work mostly from my home office unless I am traveling. Without a long commute to work, and now that our teenagers drive themselves to school, I have reset my mornings to begin with some refreshing devotional time. Our family's early mornings are energetic and fun, and the quiet house after they leave gives me just the right amount of 1st gear time to make the rest of the day productive. I would, however, like to add in more exercise because, while I don't like to do it, I do feel better about myself afterwards, which is a type of recharge for me.

Because I am an extrovert, I have realized that I need time with people who bring me to life. Most of my time is helping other people around the world via video calls, which is inspiring to me, but I also need time face to face with friends like Lance Humphreys, Bond Payne, Matthew Myers, and Ryan Litz who challenge me to think bigger.

Even more, I have realized that I need to have video calls with leaders from around the world to be able to test out ideas. My recharge, then, is a combination of introverted inspiration and extroverted ideas in fun, social environments, such as movies, themed parties, or double dates.

My wife, Kelly, on the other hand, is an introvert who enjoys exercise, reading, and time alone. We have worked hard over the years to learn how each other recharges to help that happen more often than not.

If I have too much introverted time on my own, for instance, I begin to feel drained, as if I am out of touch with people. Too much extroverted time with others and I feel like I am not disciplined and, thus, I feel out of control. Notice I used "feel" here. I know myself well enough to know that as a feeler I need to manage my feelings, as they are a key part to my leadership and the way I live.

Steve shares how he recharges and, as you will see, though we are both extroverts, our recharges are a bit different: "As someone who loves work and strategy, I have had to work hard to find activities that can override my brain's desire to keep solving complex problems and stay in 4th gear. For me, 1st gear is exercise: I enjoy the physical challenge as I get time to myself and I am able to process what I am thinking through fitness. Golf is another area of 1st gear, as I find that when I compete against myself in a beautiful setting, it motivates me. Movies also are a source of 1st gear recharge. I love the experience: I cry, I laugh, I think, I pray. A good film stays with me and I take the lessons or inspiration from it into my life. It reminds me of why I am doing what I do and refocuses my determination to be the best I can be."

What about you? Can you commit to learning more about yourself? Will you work to know yourself and then lead yourself for your benefit and for those you lead? We have more resources in the back of this book to help you know yourself better, but it starts with a commitment to recharge and rest.

Rest as Your Secret Weapon

I have a friend who really knows how to use rest well. He starts his year by building rest into his calendar. He first blocks off one day each week for a rest day (normally Sundays). He then takes one day a month and blocks it off as a focused rest day, and then a weekend each quarter for intentional rest (some days overlap). On top of that, he and his wife schedule family vacations that are a mix of 1st, 2nd, and 3rd gears.

When I shared with him that I didn't think that his calendar approach was realistic for me (he is older, in a different season, and seemingly not as busy as I currently am), he grinned and said, "Jeremie, I have been doing this for over 10 years and, no offense, but I am probably as or more busy than you." He wasn't being sarcastic, but rather challenging in a nice way. He was right. He prioritizes his rest and his life shows it.

My friend also notes that rest can give us a competitive advantage. Our 1st gear can become a secret weapon that provides greater clarity and focus that ultimately leads to better decision making and communication. When my friend shifts up into working gears after rest, he has laser-focused clarity about what he should do and should not do, and how he should communicate or handle certain situations. When you know how to rest to recharge, you will be able to handle pressure and restore the internal rhythm that is necessary to be able to operate from a position of strength.

Working from your rest, not resting from your work, is the goal.

Does this knowledge feel like a game changer for you? It should. Reordering your world to build in time for rest will change the way you live, as long as your recharge is what you need, not what others say. You should live from who you really are. If you are an introvert, build in a rhythm of rest during the day—take a walk at lunch or go to your car for a moment of rest or recharge. If you are an extrovert, then create a portfolio of recharge options that include a mix of people and ideas and time alone. Learn to mix time and space and people to help you be the best that you can be.

Jessica Tingen from Toledo, Ohio, shares how she is beginning to understand what rest looks like. Does this sound like any of you?

> I think the biggest realization for me from the 5 Gears was that what I thought was rest was not actually restful. I believed that all time away from my full-time job (in executive compensation) was rest time. When I was asked to order the amount of time I spent most to least in each of the 5 Gears, I actually had a hard time finding any time that I spent in 1st or 2nd gear. The time I spent, when I wasn't at work, was either spent with my kids (who of course I love, but let's be honest . . . time spent with a two- and four-year-old isn't necessarily restful!) or entertaining guests with my husband.
>
> I'm an introvert, so time alone to recharge is imperative and, while I knew that, for some reason I'd thought that time with my husband and my kids was close enough to alone time to be considered restful. As I began to think about how I recharge, I had a hard time as I began to see that I wasn't truly resting. The 5 Gears required that I actually

define what each of the gears would mean in my life specifically, and helped me to determine how I need to structure my week to ensure I had the proper amount of work and rest time built in.

I now have a "family 2nd gear" time and "alone 1st gear" built into our schedule. It also gave me a language to use with my husband as we planned our week, and for accountability as we have a tendency to slip into 3rd or even 4th gear during our 2nd gear time.

Why a Day of Recharge Is Smart

What if you took one day and designated it to be a complete recharge in the same way that you recharge your phone. One hundred percent is your goal. For me, Sunday is that day. It is the day our family has chosen to recharge with each other and personally. If there is a better day for you then by all means prioritize it.

Depending on the culture you are in, the Sabbath day, or day of rest, is usually a Saturday or a Sunday. Either way, a day of rest is strategic. You have heard that old adage that if you take the time to sharpen the axe then you will be more productive. Taking the time for rest is the key, but it must be the right rest for you.

My rest on Sundays has to do with my mind. I have tried to shift down and rest my mind on Sundays; therefore I don't send emails (most of the time) or take calls or work on my business on Sundays. Instead, I try hard to spend this time recharging my mind, since my work is actually in the creation of content and ideas. When I do this then I actually look forward to Monday. Ideas feel fresh because I rested appropriately.

Use Sunday as your day to sharpen the axe and refuel. It will also benefit the relationships in your life, and when Monday comes you will be more inspired and charged to do what it is you do.

Is Crashing Recharging?

Some of you are saying, "I rest a lot. I come home and binge on a TV series, lay on the couch, eat some food, and zone out." Is that rest? A lot of you think it is because that is all we know.

It may look like rest, but crashing is simply stalling out. You work 60-plus hours per week handling all types of issues. You then come home and deal with the family, teenage issues, or a frustrated spouse. Your diet is full of heavy carbs and sugars and you recharge with coffee and more work. Then you get sick, take a couple of days off, and literally crash. Or you schedule your crash over the weekend and never get out of your comfortable clothes.

Crashing is not resting; it is actually just crashing.

For some of you, I just painted what, on the surface, looks like a brilliant picture of rest. In reality, this is a horrible way to live. True rest allows you to come fully alive. Following the battery-recharging kind of rest, you smell the roses, notice the birds, feel the air, and enjoy your relationships. True, healthy rest restores you so you can continue being the best you. When you crash, as in the dismal scenario above, the fog never really lifts.

Here's another way to look at this idea: Have you noticed that when you allow your phone to lose all power that it takes quite a while for it to fully charge and function well again? The same is true for you and me. When we crash hard, we reach a place where we have completely depleted our resources. Rebounding from that sabotage takes longer than if we recharge more regularly. Proactive rest is the answer.

You have heard the statement before, "Work hard, play hard." People who use that a lot have basically been rationalizing their workaholism by scheduling an amazing vacation to reward all of those who have had to put up with them throughout the year. It is a "feast or famine" approach laced with inconsistencies.

Crashing is not resting; it is actually just crashing. Crashes cause pain, create drama, and cost money. It also causes everyone else in your world to change their patterns of living to deal with helping you pick up the pieces. What if, instead, we focused on consistent recharging that would allow us to be present with those around us?

How Leaders Can Schedule Rest

For me, I live by my calendar. Whatever is on it, I do. For some of you that is not the case. However, I would encourage anyone who has a tight schedule to start with rest. Book it. Schedule your rest day; whatever day is the best for you. Then look at your month or quarter and build some rest into your calendar.

Plan also to schedule 1st gear time into your day. When will you do 1st gear in the mornings? Do you need to downshift over lunch? What does it look like in the evening? How much sleep will you get? Asking and answering these questions is how you win long term. Building in rest makes you more productive in the everyday work of life.

Read how Nataliya Moshkovskaya viewed first gear while growing up in the Ukraine.

When I grew up, I was taught, "rest is a change of activities." If you were doing your homework for a while, cleaning the floor would be a restful occupation. If you were working in the office all day, coming to a "dacha" to dig potatoes was considered a recreation. And we did have a good time when we were doing hard physical labor together as a family.

However, our life was basically the moving from one activity to another. I can see the historical pattern in retrospection, and I know that for most of my adult life I have been doing the same thing without giving it another thought. Did I learn how to really rest? It was not even a question in my mind—I was resting all the time by changing different types of activities.

My personality probably did not help either, as I am a thinker. My sister would say, "You need to learn how to rest," but I never took it as important advice.

It was not until I learned about the 5 Gears that I finally took it seriously, because it touched my consciousness. I was horrified, not so much about the fact that I did not know how 1st gear worked or did not know how to rest, but mostly because I did not let anyone else in the close circle of my care enjoy their lives either. Here is an example: A couple of days a week I get up at 5 A.M. to go to a gym to exercise. Because I tend to have my entire day, sometimes years planned ahead, I come back from exercising at 6:30 A.M. to my house, where everyone is barely awake and I start executing my plans. I tend to get upset that they are not in the same gear as I am. My family wanted to please me, so they would respond, but it was stressful and exhausting for them.

After learning about 5 Gears and seeing from the outside how my behavior affected my family and our relationships, I had to learn and am still learning to rest and be present with the most treasured people in my life *without an agenda*. I am enjoying the changes and, as strange as it sounds, we are better friends now.

My dear husband, even after I have learned 5 Gears and started implementing them, would, before joining me for a cup of morning tea, ask me, "Do I need to be alert or can I just be?" I choose the last one—just be!

So, how would I change the definition of rest now? "Rest is when you enjoy people around you without an agenda and let both them and yourself just be."

What a great definition of rest! By implementing the 5 Gears Nataliya was able to review her past, make some changes, and affect her future with herself and those around her. What changes are in front of you?

Is 1st Gear Worth It?

So is 1st gear worth it? To know the answer, we must first ask what life looks like without 1st gear?

- Waking up in 4th gear to emails
- Being consumed by the tasks of the day, all day and all night
- Going into 5th gear mode for most of the day, while missing out on most of the interaction with others
- Coming home in 4th gear and remaining there until bedtime

- Missing interactions, relationships, and, most importantly, rest
- Eventually crashing because of the pace of work and life in 4th gear

We can only present the facts as we have experienced and discovered them. We believe that adding the proper recharge patterns into your life restores the appropriate balance in a hectic life, not to mention providing physical health and peace in a leader's life. You have to decide for yourself if you are convinced. Hear what Amy Norton, a GiANT senior associate in Nashville, says to makes her case of why 1st gear is important:

> As an introvert and a nurturer, my big a-ha with 5 Gears has been the realization that it is mission-critical to have time in 1st gear. Discovering how my personality and leadership voice dovetail with 5 Gears has transformed how I structure my rest time each day. Given my tendency to take care of other's needs before my own, I'm learning to find time to be in first gear each day. When I make it a priority to downshift and go for that walk, pick up the novel my book club is reading, and generally take time to take care of me, everyone in all of my circles of influence—from my family to my friends to my colleagues at work—benefit. Skipping first gear, believe it or not, is actually counter-productive for me.

People miss opportunities for relationships when they skip being recharged.

If you want to become a leader worth following, then rest and recharging should be a daily and weekly priority, not a one-time occasion. Remember these points as you reflect on your own needs for rest:

- Leaders undermine their influence when they skip 1st gear
- People miss opportunities for relationships when they skip being recharged
- Health takes a hit when 1st gear is abused
- A dull axe is more draining and doesn't produce as much as if it were sharpened
- To be a leader worth following, you need to demonstrate rest well

Are you tired, weary, worn out, beaten down? It is time to learn how to rest. When you do, you will see the benefits and so will those who live and work with you.

Warning Signs: You know you have an unhealthy 1st gear if . . .

- Escapism from reality is your norm.
- Too much time is devoted to 1st gear and not connecting with others.
- You overfocus on exercise and diet.
- You get lost in a new book or new idea most of the week.
- Your personal recharge dictates everyone else's schedule.
- Your recharge time dominates the family agenda.
- Using work and studying as an excuse to avoid people.
- You binge on a TV series or computer gaming as a way to escape.
- You rely on a very small number of relationships without connecting to the broader world.

How Do You Get Healthy?

- Know your wiring and what healthy recharge looks like for you.

- Trade up your time to the most healthy activity as it relates to both relationship and your recharge.
- Put healthy boundaries around your recharge time.
- Invite others to exercise with you occasionally.
- Practice 3rd gear by widening your network of relationships.
- Learn how to expend your energy wisely—don't fear getting tired.
- Learn to value how other people recharge—avoid being selfish!

Key Question: How does my need and preference for personal recharge impact the lives of those around me?

The 1st Gear Challenge

Ask someone you trust to appropriately schedule your recharge with and for you.

9 | ⚙

Reverse—Being Responsive in a Resistant World

One of the best TV shows available is a British show called *Top Gear*. It is funny, informative, and a bit crass—all the makings for mindless entertainment. One of my favorite episodes highlighted a three-wheeled car called the Reliant Robin, made by a U.K. car manufacturer in the 1970s.

There are numerous issues with a three-wheeled car, especially with the Reliant Robin. First, it was hard to turn, especially sharply. Second, it wasn't very wide, as it needed to hold the weight of the vehicle on one front wheel. Third, and most importantly, this vehicle on the show could not back up—it didn't have a reverse gear (or the reverse gear in the vehicle they were using was not working). Nonetheless, a car with no reverse would be difficult to drive and require a strategic eye when parking. Luckily, the Reliant Robin was lightweight and could be easily pushed back by a person or two.

In our 5 Gears metaphor, if vehicles represent people, then how many Reliant Robins are out there in the world, people who are not very nimble, whose lives are easily upended, and who do not have the ability to reverse, back up, and apologize. That sounds awful. To not have the ability to back up is like living with your right hand tied behind your back. And yet, millions of people live like this every day.

Reverse is a great gear. Having it in your car gives you the ability to parallel park or to hook up a trailer or fit into a tight spot. Without reverse, a driver is severely impaired. My family likes to boast about our ability to back up. That sounds funny, but my grandfather and dad both have shared memories of winning "backing up" ribbons from the county fair. I, too, think that I hold the genes of being a good "reverser," as if that is something to put on a resume. To translate this into leadership language, reverse simply means to back up, pull back, or apologize—to be responsive.

Do You Know How to Apologize?

Do you know how to apologize? That is a funny question, isn't it? Asking this might even sound a bit demeaning. What I really mean is, have you learned the etiquette of apologizing to others when you make a mistake? Did your mother and teachers embed this simple concept in your younger years? More importantly, do you mean it when you say it? It is rather

Can you admit your mistakes and ask forgiveness? Do you know how to do this?

an art form, I think, and to master this (which you completely can) you need a few skills in your back pocket.

When our kids were younger we were constantly refereeing between the three of them. "He hit me," was a consistent phrase we heard in our house. When we would ask one of our children to apologize to each other they would give the obligatory "I'm sorry," and then move on to the next activity. We think they began to understand social intelligence and the boundaries of right and wrong, but it really comes down to whether or not a child is responsive or resistant. The same goes for adults.

There are two types of people—responsive and resistant. You hire responsive ones and fire the resistant. Responsive people are self-aware and have a consciousness that is not steeped in victim mentality, but rather in responsibility. They understand that they are responsible for their actions and will make amends when they have clearly overstepped their bounds. Responsive people are the best employees, and spouses, and children.

Resistant people, on the other hand, are exhausting. They hate to admit their mistakes and will more easily pass the blame than admit a fault. Resistance is basically pride, which shows itself as insecurity. These people do not want to appear weak, so they would rather exasperate others than get to the peace that comes from admission. Resistance will fight rather than resolve, blame rather than admit, and run away rather than run toward reconciliation.

> Responsive people are self-aware and have a consciousness that is not steeped in victim mentality, but rather in responsibility.

Through the years I have had the privilege of hiring dozens of executive leaders, and my strategy for finding the gems is to look for responsiveness. When I sense resistance I nicely finish the meeting and move on to another candidate. Hiring a resistant person is not worth the drama that inevitably follows.

Admitting mistakes is a fundamental part of being responsive. When you find a responsive person you will find someone with deep character and a person to build companies or initiatives around.

What Reverse Does to Influence

Have you ever seen a professional sporting event where a player makes an obvious mistake, but immediately points to teammates to shift the blame? Their words echo, "Man, what were you thinking? Why didn't you. . . ?" That is a strategy of the resistant: shifting blame, getting the negative spotlight off of himself or herself and on to someone else. The problem with this is that in professional sports millions of people see through the replay that the initial player indeed was wrong, but now looks like the fool in front of the fans.

Conversely, have you ever noticed what happens when another player makes a mistake and then immediately pounds their chest and lifts their hand with an impassioned "my bad." The athlete just admitted his mistake in front of millions. In this scenario normally what occurs is that the player who admitted his mistake gets grace and mercy from the fans and a rallied support from the other players. You can almost read their lips as they support the guilty player. "It's okay, keep your head in the game. It will be okay." Responsive players get the respect of the team and the fans, while the resistant players lose respect from their fans and the team.

Influence rises when people admit their mistakes, unless of course they make the same mistake consistently (in this case a different type of jeering occurs). People respect people who admit their mistake and then hustle to do better next time. People do not respect others who refuse to own it when they mess up and continue to blame others. Respect, then, is gained or lost directly by the way we apologize or not.

So what causes some of us to be responsive and others resistant?

Why Self-Preservation Undermines Influence

Self-preservation undermines our ability to influence others. We could actually spend a lot of time on this. (In fact, a lot more has been written on self-preservation in my book *Making Your Leadership Come Alive*.) However, to dive a bit into understanding the basics of self-preservation will help us process why some people can apologize and be responsive and why others cannot.

The pressure in our society is on us to collect, aggregate, and protect what we have earned and what "is rightfully mine." Self-preservation is a natural tendency to protect what we are afraid of losing. Thus, if we are afraid of losing our jobs, then we will work to do whatever it takes to not lose the job. That fear of losing can cause us to become irrational and overwork a situation or relationship in order to preserve what we have. This happens all the time and can be analyzed in our own lives by answering these three questions:

1. What are you trying to prove?
2. What are you trying to hide?
3. What are you afraid of losing?

When you try to preserve yourself, defensive walls of pride pop up, which keep others from seeing the good sides of you. Instead they come up against a prickly, oversensitive person who is full of guarded talk, sarcasm, and impatience. This, then, leads to people running from you not toward you, as well as diminishing returns where respect is concerned. Influence in this instance dissipates, and you undermine yourself in the pursuit of protection.

Influence rises when people admit their mistakes.

Fear Is a Killer

Ironically, the end result of all this self-preservation is death; relationships cannot survive long term this way. All self-preservation is based on fear, which prevents us from being fully present with others because we are consumed with ourselves and our own insecurity.

I painfully remember a season when I completely undermined my own influence. We had just bought John Maxwell's events and content entity, Injoy, and merged it into our GiANT operations. I had just turned 35 and was full of myself in a lot of ways. We were in the middle of planning a Catalyst Conference event when I was asked to come to a creative meeting and just say a few words. My problem was that I wanted everyone to know who we were and that I was in charge, a very immature and insecure thing to do. So, I began by sharing my experiences as I worked to prove how much I knew about the business and why I was worthy to be leading the charge.

As I talked, you could just feel the people in the room cringing and thinking, "Really? Did you need to go there?" Afterward I felt weird as I reflected on what I had done. I wanted to establish myself and thereby allowed my insecurity to take over and make a mess of my influence. The truth was that I did not need to say a thing, but instead, if I had allowed my actions to take over, if I had simply served my team, then my influence would have grown exponentially. That struggle lasted for many years as I was trying to manage a lot of egos, brands, and events.

What fears are killers for you that lead you to put up walls of self-preservation? Ponder this list, and circle the ones that tend to cause the most damage in your life:

- Fear of being left out
- Fear of not being valued
- Fear of being embarrassed
- Fear of losing respect
- Fear of losing control
- Fear of failing in front of others
- Fear of being proved wrong
- Fear of not being known
- Fear of your ideas being rejected

All of these fears do nothing but keep you from your best. They steal your influence, kill your confidence, and destroy your relationships as they create a wedge between you and those you lead in your life. I know firsthand how damaging this can be, and I also know how secure I became when I took a sledgehammer to the walls I had built around myself.

Secure Confidence Wins

Security is a gift. The most secure people I know are normally calm, cool, and collected. When you know what you are good at and what you are not good at, then you can settle into your strengths and delegate the areas where you are least effective.

Security also breeds confidence. One of the best leaders I know understands that he is best at apprenticing young leaders and molding them in the college environment. He has great successes in the business ranks and has dabbled in the start-up world, but at the end of the day, because of his security in who he is and confidence in his role on earth, he has refocused on what he is the best in the world at—apprenticing young men and women in a university setting to become world changers. I was one of the first young, eager students whom he mentored and his guidance made a huge difference in my life. This secure and confident man poured secure confidence into me and helped me and other partners start our first business in Moscow in 1993. I am indebted to him and proud to know him.

When you are confident and secure, then you can step into roles that others may see as unglamorous or unfulfilling. Secure people can take a role in the small company rather than the large corporation; start a small nonprofit because of the mission burning in their hearts and choose things that are humble rather than boasting. Secure and confident leaders are truly humble at heart, as they are not trying to prove themselves to anyone. They are who and what they are and they have nothing to hide. Therefore, they can move confidently into what they were made to do and enjoy the fruits of their hard work in peace.

Secure, confident people are those that people want to follow. Humble leaders are responsive and therefore have more time to be present with others as they are more focused on serving others than on being served.

People are enamored with confidence, security, authenticity, and transparency. Think about the people you are most impressed with. Do they have any of the attributes above?

> *Secure, confident leaders are those that people want to follow.*

To be authentic and transparent is to be real. People like real people. If you want to increase your influence then I implore you to become more transparent, and to do that you must learn how to apologize and use your reverse gear.

How to Say I Am Sorry

It is hard to say "I'm sorry." That was a popular Chicago song from the late 1980s and, yes, I realize I have just dated myself, but it is true nonetheless. Because of our natural personality tendencies, some of us have a hard time saying this, so we will slow down for a moment, put our car in reverse, and practice. (No fair skipping to the next chapter here.) Take a deep breath and say these three words out loud: "I am sorry!" They are not menacing. Try it again, you can do it! I am being funny here, but my point is that it is really that easy to insert this phrase into your life. It might be even more helpful to give you some scenarios where you can imagine incorporating this relationship repair response:

- When your spouse says something that is hard to hear but true, take the time to pause, thank them for their comment, and say, "You are right; I do that often. Will you forgive me?" Once you pick them up off the floor you can hand them a copy of this book and ask them to read this section.
- When you are overly harsh with your kids because you are busy and they are loud, stop, gather them, and apologize like this: "Kids, I am so sorry for blowing up. Will you forgive me? I have been stressed at work and just need a little calmness tonight."
- If a co-worker infringes on your turf and you blow up with some inappropriate sarcasm, quickly learn how to apologize with a brief, "Susan, I am sorry I blew up. I'm working on getting better at communicating. My sarcasm was uncalled for and I apologize."

Every vehicle needs to be able to back up. Without reverse, a car is not worth much. Neither are leaders. If you learn the art of backing up well, you will learn how to traverse the hardest roads ahead of you and the most complex relationships.

Learn the skills of reverse and add them to your gears to become a secure, confident, humble, responsive leader.

Warning Signs: You know you have an unhealthy reverse gear if . . .

■ You use apologizing as a way to get what you want.
■ Self-deprecation or false humility is consistent in your communication.
■ You use apologies to manipulate other people.

How Do You Get Healthy?

■ Understand what a sincere apology looks like.
■ Don't over-apologize, but be clear and concise and authentic.
■ Use a journal to write down what you have learned. Reverse should lead you to epiphanies on your character or competency so that you don't continue making the same mistakes.

Key Question: What would happen in a key relationship if you started being responsive by taking responsibility for your actions and apologizing where appropriate? What would the other person do?

The Reverse Challenge

Make a list of people in your life and see if there is anything that you need to do to restore the relationship and be responsive.

10

Ranking Your Gear Order

Now that you know the full meaning behind the metaphor, it is time to start applying the 5 Gears in your life. In this section, we will help you discover your personal gear order, your gear order under stress, and the gear order of others in your life.

As I noted at the outset of this book, every vehicle has a natural gear order. For cars that order is 1st to 2nd to 3rd to 4th to 5th and reverse when you need it. Transmissions are designed to allow for an engine to be in the right gear in the right time. The same is true of people. We have a natural gear order that is meant to be, and one that is our reality.

What Is Your Gear Order?

So, what is your real gear order? Not what you want it to be, but what it actually is in your everyday life. Steve and I thought it would be good to share what our gear order is to help you understand how to think through your own. Let's start with Steve's gear order, which is 4, 1, 3, 5, 2:

> I love 4th gear: I enjoy the multifaceted nature of work. I am constantly moving between email, Facebook, iMessage, tasks, phone calls, coffees, and GoToMeeting video-conferences. I thrive on variety, autonomy, and the freedom to work from wherever I am in the world. I tend to work in bursts of energy and move in and out of work throughout the day. I love what I do, so it's actually recreation for me to dream about how we win in the future!
>
> 1st gear is next. I truly recreate when the external stimuli are more powerful than the desire to solve problems. Golf competition in a beautiful environment is 1st gear for me. I love the physical and mental challenge of competing, and the combination allows me to stay in the moment. Movies have the same effect; I find them inspiring, engaging, and thought provoking. Movies override my default to 4th gear as my brain is fully engaged in the experience unfolding on the screen.
>
> 3rd gear is next in my gear order. When I'm not overtired I really enjoy social settings, meeting new people, connecting, and sharing ideas. I love the challenge of putting people at ease, and 3rd gear gives me the chance to be charming and engaging. I have to watch the tendency to move from 3rd to 4th gear and not come back. The more

tired I am the greater the tendency to default to 4th! I have to work at staying in 3rd gear but sometimes intentionally look to use 2nd gear, if only for practice.

5th gear happens, but it is harder for me. I love what gets created when I'm forced into 5th gear. However, it's not a gear I seek or find easy to access. Invariably it's either the pressure of a deadline or enforced disconnection from the wider electronic world that gets me there. Transatlantic flights bring my very best 5th gear work.

2nd gear is typically the hardest for me. I find it a challenge to be physically, emotionally, and intellectually present in the ordinariness of family life or less inspiring gatherings! My brain is always seeking intellectual stimulation, trying to solve complex problems, and shape the future. All too often I will start speaking about work-related topics when I am supposed to be in 2nd gear space. It reveals to those closest to me that I'm not truly present, but I'm working hard on this!

As for reverse, I am decent at it. I don't mind saying I am sorry if I have seen my ways and realized that I really am in the wrong. However, it is important that whoever is challenging me be accurate and factual.

Note that this was Steve's actual order, not what he hopes it will be, but what it actually is.

Now, let me share my gear order before you create your own. Mine looks like this: 4, 2, 3, 5, 1.

4th gear is my go-to gear. My tendency is to work—all the time. Because of the many different ventures I am involved in, I tend to go from one conversation to the next, and then I work to clean up the mess I have made during the day or week. That means that I am always checking my phone or squeezing in phone conversations in my car from meeting to meeting or when traveling.

2nd gear is close behind. Recalling the story I shared in Chapter 1, I have begun to work hard over the years to focus on connect time with my family and friends. My wife and I work hard to have connect times with our kids, though hard in the high school years. We try to have dinner together and make it a priority to have date nights as well. I also need some good connect time with a few dear friends quite regularly.

I enjoy 3rd gear. I am an extrovert and I love social times. Long meals are my favorite, especially since living in the United Kingdom, as they are both 3rd and 2nd gear combined. As the social planner of our family, I like to create things to look forward to and make it a habit to have something planned in advance.

5th gear is more difficult for me. Because of the projects and my tendency to float from one thing to another, I have an issue with staying focused. Writing this book forced me to schedule 5th gear time into my calendar to meet my deadlines, and while I can do it, it is very hard for me. Turning my email off and the music up helps me focus.

1st gear is my hardest gear. I don't have a traditional 1st gear because I tend to recharge with people. Because I am an extroverted feeler I can spend my time helping other people recharge more than myself, which can create problems at times. For my health and my long-term influence, I need to get better at 1st gear.

Your gear order is strategically important to your life. You need to understand your tendencies of where you spend your time or in what gears you tend to get stuck in as well as those that are harder for you to experience.

5 GEARS

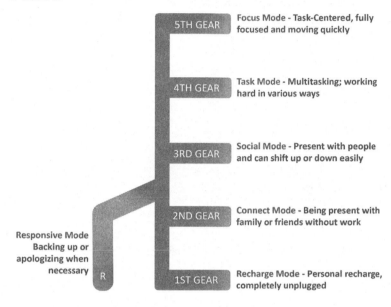

© GiANT WORLDWIDE

Figure 10.1   The 5 Gears Tool

What about you? What is your gear order? It is time to start understanding your personal gear order.

You can use the 5 Gears image (Figure 10.1) as a reminder to help you rank your gear order. Here are your instructions in order to get started.

1. Get to reality. Think about your gear order for what it really is, not what you want it to be.
2. Start from the top. Which gear is the one you are in the most?
3. Move to the bottom. Which gear is the hardest for you to hit?
4. Make the list in order from left to right with the first gear being the one you truly are in the most and the last being the hardest to get to.

5. List your gear order below.
   My Gear Order: ____, ____, ____, ____, ____

Here are some natural next questions for you to think about as you process your gear order:

- When you see this gear order, what do you think about it? How does it make you feel?
- What makes your top gear what it is? What causes it to be the highest one?
- Why is your last gear there? Why is that difficult to do well?
- Make a list of the three things that you want to change as it relates to the gears at this point in the writing.
- Lastly, who would you want to share this with? We want to challenge you to teach the gears and share your gear order with someone who is for you.

Over the past decade there has been a focus on strengths-based leadership. The basic premise of this movement is to have people focus on what a person is good at (strengths) rather than spend time on what a person is not good at (weaknesses).

As it relates to being present and learning connectivity, it is even more important that we learn to develop the gears we rank at the end (the last two). Our unconscious, or even conscious, incompetence in these gears undermines our influence with others. You cannot compensate for weaknesses in the last two gears by focusing even harder on the gears you rank highest. Therefore, it is vital that you

When you work on your weakest gear you improve your ability to influence others over time.

understand your worst gears, as they will hold the keys to improving your influence in the lives of others.

If, for example, I learn how to do 1st gear better, I will experience true rest. When I experience true rest then my family does not experience my restlessness. Rest trumps restlessness and peace comes in rest. If my 1st gear becomes settled, then it will help me more effectively order the other gears.

Gear Order Under Stress

Once you know your natural gear order, it is vital, next, to understand how your stress, whether moderate or extreme, affects you. Surely none of you get stressed, right? Your world is probably ordered with clarity and relational harmony. (Okay, I will stop with the sarcasm.)

The truth is that stress is a daily part of most of our lives. There is the moderate stress of daily living that comes from paying bills, raising kids, working, dealing with neighbors, and so on. Then there is the extreme stress that comes from meeting deadlines, dealing with sickness, or car wrecks, or bad bosses, and so on. The gears and, more specifically, our ability to connect and be present begin to break down under moderate stress and under extreme stress are actually reordered.

We contend that most moderate stress is self-induced, with most of it happening primarily because of a lack of self-awareness or a lack of being present by being in the wrong gear at the wrong time.

Stress can play tricks on your mind. It typically raises self-preservation as fears get touched like nerves as deadlines are near or expectations from others become evident. Stress can elevate thinking into irrational behavior or embellishment, which causes a ripple effect of internal and external drama with the consequences leading to relational breakdowns and disconnections.

I once worked with a CEO who felt like he was being forced out of his position. It was not actually happening, but because of his stress he began to question some of his executive team as to why they were having meetings with board members. He was becoming paranoid, and in the process tended to stay firmly in 5th gear, as he would close his door and play out his make-believe scenarios. The situation eventually came to a head with a key board member confronting the CEO and challenging him in a way that was like throwing a glass of cold water into his face. It worked.

After the intervention, the CEO shared how grateful he was for the challenge because he knew that the board member was for him. He was quite embarrassed at what he saw in himself. His stress had caused his self-preservation to stir up his fear. Fear, then, became the driver and caused him to shift into an unhealthy 5th gear as he obsessed over things that were beyond his control.

Interestingly, the CEO found out that the board was indeed interviewing his key executives about his performance because they wanted to give him a raise, not to fire him. Fear caused those conversations to cease and instead of positive remarks, the CEO received a challenge.

Irrational behavior can strike any of us. Stress actually increases the chances. When we are under moderate stress, our gear order begins to break down a bit, while under extreme stress our gear order becomes disordered. And in stress mode we have noticed that people will tend to either scurry to 4th or 5th gear, or retreat or hide in 1st or 5th gear.

So, what gears do you normally gravitate toward when experiencing both moderate and extreme stress? Let's look at Steve's and my gear order first:

Under moderate stress, Steve's tendencies are to lean more heavily on 4th gear, which causes him to work more. This is normally caused by fatigue. His mind stays working even when he is supposed to be at rest. That reality causes him to slip from 2nd and 3rd gear back into 4th very easily.

Under extreme stress Steve naturally goes into an unhealthy 1st gear. His tendency is to withdraw from people and start to shut down by sleeping more and by watching sports. Ultimately, extreme stress causes him to become isolated, as he does not want to be around people.

Therefore, Steve's stress gears oscillate between 4th (moderate) and 1st (extreme).

My patterns for handling moderate stress are to slide into 4th gear, simply to buckle down and crank out the work. My evenings will fill up and I will use Saturdays to cover for any leftover work that was not accomplished during the week. Because I like to work, it is sometimes hard to tell what is moderate stress and what is the normal everyday reality.

Under extreme stress I tend to shift into a hurried 5th gear as I try to fix whatever problem I am facing. I suddenly become very serious and can call for battle stations, as I want everyone to know there is a problem and for us all to focus to solve it. Under stress I work more, not less. My communication suffers as I become short with people, demanding a lot via email or text. This reality is not much fun for those around me;

in this state I can also have the tendency to blame others for the issues or defer blame in some contexts.

The problem with this pattern is that I can lose respect or influence with people, especially when I did not share expectations and move from being the rah-rah guy to a dominator. While I do not like this about myself, I know that it can happen. Thus, I begin to lead myself out of these situations or preemptively keep myself away from this stressful pattern if at all possible.

My stress gear pattern is 4th (moderate) and 5th (extreme). Where do you tend to slide under moderate and extreme stress? Consider it, and jot your answers below for future reference:

My Stress Gear (moderate) = _____
My Stress Gear (extreme) = _____

Introvert/Extrovert Gear Order

As we share the 5 Gears across the globe, we are noticing the differences between personality preferences as it relates to gear order.

It appears that introverts generally have a much easier time of being in 1st and 5th gears, which makes sense, as those gears are full focus or full recharge gears. It is often much easier for introverts to recharge by being in their minds or having time to reflect. Both 1st and 5th gears are less people-oriented and lend themselves to giving introverts the internal battery recharge they need.

Extroverts, on the other hand, tend to like 4th, 3rd, and 2nd gears much more because of the people interaction and ability to move around inside relationships. If you are an extrovert, you should not be surprised that you tend to stay in these gears and have a harder time with either the 5th gear focus or the 1st gear recharge.

As I mentioned earlier, my tendency as an extroverted feeler is to be in 4th, 3rd, and 2nd gears because I also recharge in those gears and am always making sure my family is in a good spot before I focus on any alone time. My wife, conversely, is an introverted thinker and needs time alone or to run errands where she is not needing to use words or energy with others. She loves to work on a project by herself in 5th gear or get time to read or exercise alone in 1st.

Understanding Others' Gear Order

Understanding your personal gear order is vital for you in your growth to be a leader others want to follow. Understanding others' gear order is a gift for everyone. When you can begin to live your life learning to support others based on who you are and who they are, then you have begun to master what it means to be a leader, and your influence will begin to soar.

The 5 Gears are easy to understand and teach. We suggest you help people understand their gear order and where they slide under stress in order to more effectively know what their tendencies are and how to help them lead and live more effectively.

Start with yourself, then help your family understand their gear order by sharing yours. Take it to your teams and then your whole organization. In the remaining chapters we will be highlighting many practical ways to incorporate the tool in your life. At this stage, we want you to simply be aware of others' gear tendencies as they relate to you, and you to them.

SECTION THREE

Living and Leading Connected

11 | ⚙

Master Your Settings—Right Time, Right Place

We laugh when we see the bumbling idiot, played by a daft comedian, enter a scene at the wrong time, saying things in the wrong way to the wrong people. Peter Sellers, Jim Carrey, and Will Ferrell have perfected emotionally incorrect characters. And yet we all know these same characters in the everyday script of our lives.

By using the 5 Gears appropriately, you can minimize being in the wrong in relationships, conversations, and situations if you understand time and space. What I mean is that there is an appropriate time to have certain conversations and certain places to which a certain topic should or shouldn't be discussed. This is both emotional intelligence and social etiquette wrapped into one. Learning this requires a mind shift, unless of course you want to mimic the goofball characters played on the big screen.

So how do you take what we have learned thus far and begin to make the changes that could positively affect you and those around you the rest of your life? Let's start with time.

The Right Time

Have you ever arrived at an appointment an hour early, or worse, an hour late? It is a frustrating feeling when you have realized that you have done the right thing at the wrong time. Your intention was correct, but your clock was off. Time is a critical aspect of life. Comedians get paid millions for their timing. UPS and FedEx charge more for accurate delivery. Airplanes and movies and churches and meetings run on time.

However, time is more than a number. It also entails seasons. There is a right time for a challenging conversation and a wrong time for one. This includes the actual time as well as the right mood or time for the conversation.

There is an appropriate time for everything. To increase your ability to connect, then you must know what season or time you are in before you communicate. That knowledge leads you to knowing yourself, leading yourself, and then shifting into the appropriate gear at the appropriate time.

Everyone's day is different and yet the patterns are the same. We all wake up and go to sleep. We must eat and drink to survive, so we have our rhythm of meals. Most of us have some sort of work that we do either at a location or at home each day. We also tend to have some social contact with customers, friends, family, and so on.

Taking this into account, here is a version of a normal day for those going to an office job. I realize that the times will be different for each of us, but for the purpose of illustration, this example gives you an idea of how to tie the time of day with your gears.

6 A.M.—Wake Time—1st Gear
7 A.M.—Drive Time—1st or 4th Gear
8 A.M.—Work Time—4th or 5th Gear
12 Noon—Lunchtime—3rd or 1st Gear
1 P.M.—Work Time—4th or 5th Gear
5 P.M.—Drive Time—4th or 1st Gear
6 P.M.—Dinner Time—2nd or 3rd Gear
8 P.M.—Social Time—3rd or 2nd or 1st Gear
10 P.M.—Bedtime—1st Gear

As you can see, there is a natural time for the gears. Morning time should not start in 4th gear, just like a car shouldn't begin there either. We need to warm up before we shift up to drive through our day.

We recognize that the above schedule is not everyone's schedule. Some of you wake up much earlier and some later, while others of you are laughing at the idea of leaving the office at 5 P.M. This is a basic schedule to start the conversation and paint a picture of what choosing the right gear at the right time looks like.

Every time I speak on the 5 Gears and discuss time, I am asked to share what a possible schedule might look like for a stay-at-home spouse whose work is centered on home and children. Here is my attempt:

6 A.M.—Wake Time—1st Gear
7 A.M.—Breakfast—4th Gear
8 A.M.—Project/Kids School or Play Time—4th or 5th Gear
12 Noon—Lunchtime—3rd, 4th or 1st Gear

1 P.M.—Project or Nap Time for kids—4th or 5th Gear

5 P.M.—Dinner Prep Time—4th Gear

6 P.M.—Dinner Time—4th Gear with hopes of 2nd Gear

8 P.M.—Rest Time—4th Gear or hard 1st Gear

10 P.M.—Bedtime—1st Gear

Does this resemble your life or your spouse's life at all?

The key here is to learn how to shift appropriately into the right roles as we put other hats on for the day. For instance, if I am responsible for many people in a given day, then come home to the equal amount of responsibility, I am going to simply stay in 4th or 5th gear. If, on the other hand, I understand that I can downshift into 2nd because that is what my family wants or needs, then I really need to practice doing that.

Time itself has a pressure on it. Lunchtime normally leads to more social space in 3rd gear, whereas work should be more of a 4th and 5th gear space. When you know the time that you are in, then you have an advantage in understanding how to shift and where to be present.

Here is an exercise that can make this concept come to life.

1. Map your schedule. Take a piece of paper and draft your normal schedule as it really is. Write down when you wake up, go to work, and so on.
2. Add your gears. Beside each time, list the gears you tend to be in based on time. Take a look at what this means. Are you seeing any patterns that are preventing you from connecting well? Are there places where you are in the wrong gear at the wrong time of day?
3. Adjust. Now list the actual changes that should be made. If you wake up and go into 4th gear, cross it out and replace with 1st.

4. Share your schedule. Show someone to validate that it is reality and discuss the changes that need to occur.

Time is crucial. When we are in the wrong gear at the wrong time, we create disconnections with all those we are around at that moment. Know the time; shift to the gear that is appropriate. Family time around dinner can be 2nd gear easily, if you are intentional. If you are sitting at the dinner table with your eyes locked on to your smartphone then are you surprised that you have lost your influence with your children or spouse? The only one you are connected with at that moment is your technology or the person on the other end of their tether. Disconnect to connect.

This may require you to change your schedules dramatically or change your mindset in order to get into the right frame of mind and be present with others.

> When we are in the wrong gear at the wrong time, we create disconnections with all those we are around at that moment.

The Right Place

Just as we need to consider time in terms of our gears, so, too, do we need to consider place. 4th and 5th gears are appropriate for work, whether that is in a home or an office, but when we are in 4th gear at the dinner table or in the bedroom it creates havoc. In the same way, 3rd gear with friends is designed for a social setting at an appropriate time. Have you ever had an experience where someone enters a 3rd gear time, whether at a dinner or a fun social setting, and yet brings their 4th and 5th gear office world with them? Mr. Kill Joy! It feels odd. We shift in our seats and try to listen or speak to them about their topic for a bit. Over time people flee these types by moving seats or turning their heads away from the person who has not learned how to connect with people in the right time and in the right space.

Because we work with leadership teams in many different sectors and countries, we get to see quite a bit of drama and interesting behavior. One of our programs is called a Team Intensive, which basically aligns people to each other and to the vision of the CEO. Every time we create the list of who should be involved there is always one guy that gets the eye roll. They know they need to invite him, but they would rather file paperwork than be around him. Why? Precisely because that person tends to say the wrong things at the wrong time and creates unwanted drama.

It is so very important to understand who you are with, what you should say, especially as it relates to the location.

Places and time are tied together. Breakfast restaurants are usually not open for dinner. Romantic dinner spots are not open for breakfast. Drive-in movies were built for nighttime. Places have a natural meaning for the type of connection around a specific time. What types of connection and which gears come to mind when you think of the following places:

- A Starbucks coffee shop?
- An office?
- The golf course?
- A concert?
- The romantic restaurant?
- A hotel?
- A playground or park?
- A church?

When a person enters these places in the wrong way they immediately start in a negative position and often are not aware of it. If you start off a relationship in a negative position it is always hard to get to a strong positive impression. A romantic restaurant, for example, is made for handholding, not spreadsheets. If the person remains in the wrong gear in the wrong time in the wrong place then they begin to quickly lose influence and connectivity. Ultimately they receive a negative reputation that causes others to stay away, while the culprit is clueless about what is really happening.

> The secret to being present is to learn how to shift gears appropriately in time and place in order to connect well.

5 Circles of Influence

To help you understand what gear you should be in it is important to look at certain levels of influence (Figure 11.1). We have found that there are five circles of influence that we all tend to move in and out of. These circles constitute both time and place. Some of us have learned how to move in and out of these circles with ease, while others continue getting stuck in knowing how to move in and out appropriately.

The circles begin with the way you view yourself. Next is family. Family could include the extended family or nuclear family or a collected group of friends that play the role of family. Team, which follows family, could include your work team or a group of people you work closely with. I know one entrepreneur who has no employees and never sees his customers, but has inserted two other vendors into his life as part of his team to serve

5 CIRCLES OF INFLUENCE

Figure 11.1   GiANT 5 Circles of Influence

his clients. The organization is the broader company and its influence. For instance, you might work for a division or a team, but get paid by an association or a company. Lastly, community could include a neighborhood, an area, or a specific city.

The interesting part about the five circles of influence is that most of us have compartmentalized each one. We could be one character type to our family, a different person at work, and an entirely different person to the community. The key to long-term respect and sustainable influence is for you to become consistent throughout all five circles.

Each circle of influence affects the other. For example, I know a couple, both work, and they have a disabled teenager who requires a full-time nurse. This family situation affects all five circles of influence because of the mental, physical, and emotional needs of the entire family. Because they have been living like this for 18 years they have become cognizant of the gears and have done a better job than most of shifting into the right gear at the right time.

What Is Your Approach to Connecting?

There is a right way to connect with people and a wrong way to connect with people. Those wanting to improve their emotional intelligence and increase their ability to connect must learn what is appropriate in time, space, and style.

Let's get a bit more descriptive in what we are discussing here.

- There is a right time to ask someone how he or she is doing and mean it.
- There is an appropriate time and style to bring a challenge to someone, and email is not that vehicle.
- There is a best way to talk about work with your spouse or kids.
- There is a proper style and time to bring up a big issue with your boss.

The appropriate comment spoken in love during a period of grief can lift the soul and make an impact for life. Conversely, the awkward comment spoken at the wrong time in the wrong way can ruin a reputation for years.

The word of encouragement shared at the right time can cause people to fill journals and change lives forever, whereas the casual sarcastic comment at the wrong time can take the legs off the person you are talking to.

No one is perfect. We all miss the mark in some ways. This book is written to help equip you to get better, to know where to practice to become more socially and emotionally adept. The 5 Gears are designed to give you a practical language as a reminder to yourself and others to connect.

Putting It Together

Imagine getting so good at the gears that you begin to shift correctly into the right one at the right time. What if you could move in and out of your day with ease, connecting with people in the proper way? What would that do to your emotional stability and your internal peace? Wouldn't it be great if people were consistently glad to see you, because they know you know how to engage?

Brian, a great leader living in Michigan, was having difficulty untethering from the demands of work. He was finishing his PhD, working during the day, as well as coaching others on the side. That amount of activity during the day made it so difficult for him to shut down at night that he simply stayed in 4th and 5th gear from seven in the morning to 10 at night, and then aptly crashed hard into 1st gear, only to start again the next day.

He learned about the 5 Gears and began to implement them in his life, sharing it with his wife and kids. One day, after returning home from work, he was out on his porch carrying on a conversation with a colleague on his phone when his son knocked on the window and held up two simple fingers in the form of a V. It was 2nd gear time and Brian's son knew it. The only person who forgot was Brian. Brian then quickly finished the call, turned off his phone, and shifted gears.

Brian got caught being in the wrong gear at the wrong time on something that could have been discussed easily the next day. When you are in 4th and 5th gear nonstop it is very difficult to get out of those gears and shift unless you have practiced, set up your markers (which we will discuss in the next chapter), and implemented.

You can learn how to be yourself and add value in relationships. You can actually improve your ability to connect when, and only when, you become intentional about doing things differently. It is now time to lead yourself if you want to be a leader who connects well in the right time, in the right place, and in the right way.

12

Shifting Well— Learning How to Transition

It takes years of practice to learn how to shift a manual car effortlessly. It requires a good ear to understand when to shift, hand-eye coordination to shift to the proper gear, and the use of your left foot to push in the clutch, which allows the gears to align and slide into the right slot. Shifting well, then, is both an art and a science.

Most North Americans drive automatic vehicles these days, which do the shifting work for us, so we miss out on this experience on the road, but not in our lives. All of our relationships require us to learn how to shift and shift well. Over time, as our relational shifting skills improve, what begins as a methodical, potentially awkward, step-by-step process evolves to feel automatic as we become unconsciously competent at connecting and being present with those in our lives. Until we reach that place, this book can act as an owner's manual on how to connect well and increase influence and respect.

> As our relational shifting skills improve, what begins as a methodical, potentially awkward, step-by-step process evolves to feel automatic as we become unconsciously competent at connecting and being present with those in our lives.

Practice, Practice, Practice

Imagine taking an old 1963 Corvette Stingray for a spin after years of driving an automatic. I am thinking this imaginary Corvette is a two-seat roadster, manual transmission, of course. As you start the car to allow the engine to warm up, you take hold of the steering wheel with your left hand and reach with your right hand to take hold of the stick shift. Your left foot is on the clutch and your right foot is on the brake. It's time to roll. As you look for traffic on the road ahead, you put your foot on the accelerator, and then you release the clutch.

"Flump." You've just stalled the engine. It's been a while, eh? As you look at the gearshift, you realize that you started in too high a gear, and so you put the clutch in, shift to neutral, and begin again.

You restart the engine with a bit more focus than before. You are now in first gear and you rev the engine, release the clutch, and accelerate with the right foot. The Corvette begins to purr and you can hear the roar of the engine. As you hear the sound of the engine at the height of first gear, you know it is time to shift.

Your left foot presses the clutch, the right foot eases off the gas and your hand pulls down into second gear, all as you keep your eye on the road and the steering wheel straight. Just as you go through the routine you hear the "kurrr . . . kur" sound of grinding gears, which causes you to cruise in neutral until you get into gear. An hour later, after some trial and error, you finally find the rhythm of shifting correctly and can begin to enjoy the power of the great Corvette.

We know the old adage, practice makes perfect. And it's the intentional practice that allows your gear shifting to become smooth again when driving. It's an art and a science, remember. So is being present with the people in your life.

Learning to be present, learning how to shift up or down to fully connect, whether that is with your kids, or your co-workers or your boss requires the same discipline. It does not just happen: it takes practice. If you don't know that you are supposed to shift, then you have a problem.

When you begin to know what gear you should be in and what time or place you are in you can begin to practice. Start by being aware—think. Where are you? Who are you with? This is when you practice shifting in your mind. What gear should you be in at that moment? Practice!

Chad is an executive director of a national cooperative association. He has boundless energy and brings that focus and determination with him through the door every morning. Chad knows, and all those who work with him do as well, that to be under his leadership is to be challenged and supported to deliver efficient and productive work. But lately Chad has been considering the 5 Gears analogy as a way to remind himself to "put the clutch in" between different engagements. On the way to and from a meeting in his office complex, Chad is choosing to stop, even if it is just for 30 seconds, for a bit of 3rd gear engagement in the doorways of different colleagues. He doesn't naturally do 3rd gear well, but in a season of transition and growth, and with the stress that comes with it, he has come to realize that 3rd gear can be a time to add in "support." He is being intentional by adding this into the rhythm of his leadership. The simple discipline of doorway time and conversational questions like "How was the weekend?" breaks his perceived persona without compromising his commitment to excellence and achievement.

Practice with the little things and then watch how it affects the big things.

Using Markers as Trigger Points

One of the best things I have done in my life has been to create markers that trigger action in my mind. These trigger points are actually mind tricks to help me shift into a different gear. You can do this as well. These markers are vitally important to the success of the 5 Gears to achieve the desired changes you want. Here are some examples of using markers to trigger action to downshift.

1. **Picking a marker two to five miles from home as your trigger point to downshift into 2nd or 3rd gear.** My marker was a QuikTrip gas station sign two miles from my home, which in Atlanta was 10 minutes because of traffic. That marker was my "drop zone" that reminded

me it was time to wrap up phone conversations and shift into thinking about where my wife and kids were that day. I would then shift my mind, pray for them, and think about what was going on and what they needed that evening. The marker at the sign triggered me to prepare to connect with my family. If you are single, then this habit allows you to adjust to home and a different gear.

2. **Using your neighborhood sign to put your phone in your purse or bag.** When you reach your neighborhood, put your phone in a bag or purse and leave it in your car or by the front door so that your family gets you, not your phone. If you are single then this allows you to go into recharge mode, not continually 4th gear.

3. **Using the :58s as a marker.** If you have a meeting at 2:00 P.M., then use 1:58 as your marker to shift from your 4th gear activity to 3rd gear. Think about whom you are meeting and what you are trying to accomplish. When you see that person, start with 3rd gear conversation and then slide into 4th. You will notice your influence go up instead of staying glued to email and having an abrupt shift from 4th that is hard for everyone.

4. **Make a certain hour your trigger point.** If you are home with young kids during the day, choose certain hours as shifting points. "Ok guys, its nine A.M., let's get into our project or school (4th gear)." This also works to shift into 3rd or 2nd gear. "Who's ready to play before I start dinner?" Make five P.M. the marker.

5. **5th gear signs at work.** A number of leaders have created signs on their office doors or desks to let people know that they are in 5th gear. In fact, here is how Ray Griffin and his team in Oklahoma City use markers. "One of our staff implemented an 'office door' awareness idea. If their door is open, it is 3rd or 4th gear. If the door is cracked open then they are in 4th and if the door is closed then they are in full

5th gear. Because of the language and visual we know how
to respond and respect each other."

Cheryl from Atlanta shared this story with me about how
markers have changed her relationship with her son:

The 5 Gears have actually had a profound impact on my
life. After self-assessment, I realized I was in 4th gear almost
all of the time, including my time at home. I was continually checking email and conducting business calls after 5:00,
and was not devoting enough attention to my son Jack. At
six years old, he still wants my attention and loves to play
with me, but I wasn't carving out any time to devote to
him. I decided to try the technique executive core suggested and designated a spot, in my case the gas station near
my house, as a trigger spot to disengage from my business
phone/email.

I do not look at email or conduct business calls from
5:30 until my son goes to sleep at night. On the weekends, I
don't look at email until Jack goes to bed, meaning I don't
look at it during the day on Saturdays and Sundays at all.

After he is in bed I can check email, and usually do.

This has been a very difficult change for me, but the
impact of the change has been incredible, and has blessed
my son and me.

Jack and I spend much more quality time together
working on his homework, playing, cooking dinner
together, and talking. He loves it. I realized that I was
missing so much by only giving him part of my attention.
The 5 Gears have made such a positive influence in my life.

Tim in Wisconsin shifts like this: "Knowing this tool
brings awareness of where I am during each day and where

I should be at a given time. One of the ways of being aware of this tool is when I need to bring myself from 4th gear toward the end of the day to the gear I "need" to be in by the time I get home. I have a place I go past every day on my way home that reminds me to start downshifting so I am in 2nd gear. I rarely ever get to or want to be in 1st gear, but my happy place is when I am in 2nd gear."

Shifting from Work to Home

Shifting is so hard to do, but when we learn how to do it well it makes all the difference in the world. It is where life change happens, relationships improve, and more peace comes. As I was writing this book in my home office, my wife, Kelly, opened the door and told me that she had planned a picnic at the pond by our house for Valentine's Day. I wish I could tell you that shutting off work and going with her on that impromptu lunch date was easy for me. It was not. There she was, standing with a gorgeous smile and a basket full of great food, ready to be with me, and I was having a hard time shifting. What was even more amusing is that I was writing a section of this book on being present and yet I had a hard time shifting myself. I was so in my head, fully in 5th gear. Luckily I closed the computer, took my wife's hand, and walked to the pond to sit under a tree, eat the amazing food, and talk briefly about the writing and the day.

Whether you work at home or at an office, shifting our minds to being present is so very difficult.

I love how Sue from Wisconsin discusses her battle with shifting:

Back in April after our meeting I really started to make this a priority focus in my life. Since then my husband and I have communicated about the gears with aspects of both of our jobs as well as at home. It has become common language in our home. If he finds me coming home in a gear that isn't where I should be, he will say, "Honey, you're in 5th gear right now," which is exactly what I want him to do. It is important for me to continue to grow.

One evening I sat down with Craig to talk about how his work email really bothers me at night when we are home with our family. He will read an email that may change his mood for the rest of the evening. We spoke in detail about how there is no email that cannot wait until he's back at work in the morning. If someone truly needs him they will call. The gears have been allowing us to transition from work to home much easier than before. He's been working hard at leaving work at work instead of checking his email frequently at home.

Shifting well is an art and a science.

Shifting from 4th or 5th to the appropriate gear can happen, but it must be intentional and it must be practiced in order to do it well.

When Transitions Are Complex

For some of you, working at an office would be much easier as you have clearer transition points. Going from office to home should be a trigger point in and of itself. When you work from home or are a stay-at-home parent it becomes much more difficult as your house is the setting for all of the gears.

If this is your reality then it is vital to use time as trigger points and to implement the language into your family life. I once spoke to about 200 leaders in La Crosse, Wisconsin, at one of our Liberating Leader events. As I shared details about schedules and the transition points at work, I noticed a group of women who were stirring in their seats, full of comments and questions about those who stayed at home or were teaching their children. The point they were making is that their schedules and lives were more complicated than the normal family. It was quite funny as they talked about applying the gears in more complex situations. My advice was simple. Everyone is different in the way they live and work, but we have common needs—to connect, rest, and work. Therefore, know yourself and your tendencies and where you tend to reside as it relates to the gears and the gears under stress and then practice shifting for your best and those in your life.

For some of you, complexity looks like managing a divorce situation or the sickness of a family member. Whatever your situation, learning to transition well can change relational dynamics and bring peace into tough situations.

Language to Help Others Transition Well

Learning this for yourself is one thing. Helping others learn this is an entirely different opportunity for growth. It always starts with you first. When people see that you are growing and becoming more emotionally intelligent, you will gain their respect and their ear, as they listen to how you have made improvements in your own life. The power of the 5 Gears is in the language. It is a common vocabulary that can also be used as sign language if you are intentional about it.

As you have read, there are leaders, from large corporations to stay-at-home moms, who have learned how to integrate this language at work and at home. Michael Lukasewski, CEO of Church Fuel, integrated the tools within his family. I like the way he describes it:

> Creating a vocabulary for Jennie and me to use allowed us to have conversations without being defensive. "Hey babe, let's get into 2nd gear" is way better than saying, "You need to be present with the kids." The language creates objective language instead of subjective judgment.

Another leader described how he used the tools in a crisis:

> My wife and I recently used it as I encountered a crisis at work. We were out together for a day off, and I got a call about an urgent situation. I was able to say, "I have to go into 5th gear, but I will get back to 2nd gear in about two hours." She understood, I understood, and it just made it easier to communicate and respond fully to the crisis and then to return fully to our time together.

Try it. You will see. Most drama comes from subjective comments that feel like criticism. These words make our defensive pride spike with barbs or resistance and counter comments. When we become objective, clear, and concise, all of that drama and insecurity dissipates.

When people see that you are growing and becoming more emotionally intelligent, you will gain their respect and their ear as they listen to how you have made improvements in your own life.

Highlighting Your Transitions

There is a natural time to shift from 1st to 2nd and from 4th to 5th and so on. Your engine tells you, if you listen well. So does the terrain. Some of you have vehicles that even tell you when to shift gears.

After hearing so many stories and examples, what are the shift points that you need to practice, smooth out, or learn how to transition into? Here are some possible shift points to help you implement this immediately.

- **Shifting from 1st gear to the start of the day:** We would encourage you to learn what recharges you and do that before you start your work.
- **Transition from home to your office:** If you drive to work, how can you make the most of that time in 1st gear?
- **Getting into 4th and 5th well:** There are some of you who have a hard time getting into the work gears. What needs to happen to make that transition smoother?
- **Using lunch for 1st, 2nd, or 3rd gears:** Is it okay to take a break? Yes, there are times where we need to work through lunch. Long term, however, if you don't take the time to connect with others, it will have a negative affect on your health and your influence.

- **Using the :58s to shift more effectively:** Do you have issues with connecting at work? Use the two minutes before your next meeting to shift well and watch how that affects your emotional intelligence and respect.
- **Learning to shift on the way home:** Where do you need to create markers as trigger points? Is it a bridge or a sign? Trick your mind to get into the right gear for the right time.
- **Communicate the gears at home:** When you teach the language, you are affecting your culture at home. Watch what happens. Be assertive in changing the dynamics in your personal life.
- **Shifting to rest:** How can you shift into the right gear in the evenings to make you more productive the next day? Find what recharges you and invest in that time well.

Is Neutral a Gear?

We often get asked if neutral is a gear. The short answer is "no." Gears propel a vehicle or person to go either forward or backwards. Neutral is simply a transition between gears. While it is true that a car can be stationary in neutral and not moving, it is not a gear that leads to progress.

Neutral is designed for transitions, from one gear to the next. Some of us take longer to transition from one gear to the next. However, the more you practice, the smoother your transitions will become. Neutral is not a gear, but a transition to get you into the right gear at the right time.

The 5 Gears are about the application of emotional intelligence into the life of a leader. It leads to better connectivity, influence, and respect. When you learn to shift well, then you are improving your life and your leadership exponentially. However, to get the results you desire for the long term, it is imperative that you become intentional in your implementation.

13 ⚙

Intentional versus Accidental

What is the opposite of intentional? Unintentional is the obvious answer. And yet, I think a better word is accidental. Being intentional means to make things happen on purpose. Being accidental is to hope things happen by chance. Intentional living includes deliberate thoughts and plans. Accidental living, conversely, means you do not think about much. Most people live accidentally.

- They hope that their kids grow up to be responsible.
- They hope that they will have income to retire on.
- They hope that their business takes off one day.
- They hope that the new employee they hired is an all-star.

Did you notice the repetition of the word hope in the list above? With accidental living, we hold out hope as the action.

With intentional living, we hold on to hope as our motivator, but we plan and act with a purpose.

Accidental leadership is non-productive in the same way that accidental parenting is dangerous to everyone. Yet it happens every day. People hope that the teachers, the neighbors, and the grandparents will help raise their kids. People hope that the new person was hired correctly because they don't have time to train them. And hope in these cases actually really means "I wish," where we wish that all we hope for happens.

The truth is that you do not have time to not hire correctly, train your children, or apprentice the new employee. It is such a waste of money to train poorly. When we invest in people, the chances of receiving a return on investment are much higher than hoping the employee works out or the child turns out ok.

> *Accidental leadership is non-productive in the same way that accidental parenting is dangerous to everyone.*

What Does Investment Look Like?

When you invest in treating a car correctly in the short term, you are mitigating potential higher costs long term. When you create a culture where your people can thrive, it may cost you more time, energy, and money, but it will save many headaches and the higher costs that turnover normally brings.

The same goes with our families. When we are intentional in our investment of time, when we pour into the lives of those closest to us, then the chances of a great return go up dramatically. Yes, kids will make bad choices, but I stand by the fact that being present and connected with your children will have a much more positive effect than just throwing money at them or taking them on vacations once a year. They want and need you, not your things.

My dad is a great farmer. He takes immaculate care of the farm and spends hours each month planning for the future. He knows his acres like the back of his hand and he intentionally invests for the future in technology, land management, and nutrients. The yields on the farm show the payoff most years, outside of drought or major breakdowns. The secret to his farming is his intentional investment to work the land as a good steward.

Another way of saying this is that investment is intentional living. Being intentional is a way of life. Becoming self-aware will help you recognize your patterns and tendencies and make the changes necessary in order to invest in those who are in your life, whether at work or at home. Brian Hood, from Naples, Florida, knows that intentional investment reaps returns. He became aware that his baby daughter would get excited when she saw his car pull into the driveway, but then over time became less excited when she realized he would stay in his car to spend the next 20 minutes finishing up his work calls and emails. He resolved to change his ways and now leaves his cell phone in the car so he can focus on his family. He has made the changes and commitment not to miss out on being present for such a short period of time in his daughter's life. That is what it looks like to become self-aware, intentional, and present. That's intentional living.

Realizing that I wasn't being fully present and doing something about it changed my life and my relationships with my kids. After working for nearly seven years in a stressful job, a job that was not really right for me, I fired myself, hired a good leader, and moved my family to England to have intentional time together and to refine who I was and what I wanted to do. This entire book, in fact, is directly related to that decision to be intentional.

This process led to the start of the fifth GiANT company, GiANT Worldwide, with Steve Cockram, whose mission is to help people become leaders worth following and train them to build other leaders worth following in cultures that everyone wants to work in.

We moved into a historic manor built in 1583, which became a place where leaders from around the world could come and rebuild and be restored. From this place came the idea for this book as Steve and I looked at our lives and our respective families and children. Our wives began to appreciate the changes that came with the renewed investment in knowing our issues and responding to them by learning to shift and be more intentional than ever.

There are now over 50 GiANT associates in several countries helping other leaders and organizations to become more intentional in their own leadership and teaching them how to develop high potential teams and liberating cultures. We call them GiANTs because they have become secure, confident, and humble leaders who people want to follow, not have to follow. We are simply taking principles and concepts into organizations to help them become more intentional, consistent, and healthy.

Leading Your Life Intentionally

During our time in England, we had the privilege of serving leaders from around the world. At times, these leaders would bring their spouses to our retreats and we would help them implement healthy leadership in their work, families, and communities. One of our favorite experiences happened with Dr. Scott Koss and his wife Paula. As you read his story, notice the intentional change that occurred as he made being present a priority:

> What an honor to share stories from my life after our GiANT infusion! I want to share the everyday examples of how the 5 Gears concept has improved my leadership skills. You have distilled the mental and physical aspects of our waking experience to a visual concept that affords me the opportunity to coordinate my gears so that I can lead better. I have experienced this with how I lead my family, my team, and myself.
>
> First, the gears concept has prompted me to *intentionally* downshift to low-level gears prior to arriving at home from being in 4th and 5th gear all day at the hospital. Without question, being much more present has made my time with my family more connected, rich, and natural. This strategy has evolved into the institution of a Koss Family rest day each week, when we completely unplug and spend time together and with friends/family. Interestingly, outside of the natural product of relaxation, we have found that we have been able to accomplish our home tasks with greater ease. I am certain that this strategy will continue to bless our family.
>
> After my recent Leadership Intensive experience with GiANT, I have begun to intentionally schedule dedicated pioneer time. The extroverted driver in me thrives in this environment, protected from distraction, and gets me to a steady 5th gear. My creative output has been great and I expect that regularly scheduled time will take me to a level that I have yet to experience in my professional life. Thank you for introducing this intentional way to live to me.

Imagine what life would look like if your work and life and time were a bit more balanced, not only with time management skills, but also with intentional connectivity. Imagine the depths of relationships that you could experience if being present began to be a part of your everyday experience. It can happen when leaders begin to live intentionally—consistently.

See if you are not as inspired as we have been reading these next few stories of the 5 Gears at work in the lives of others. Linda Creighton, from Atlanta, Georgia, shares the benefits she received from being intentional in her life and work in the following ways:

During one season of work recently it felt like I was in 5th gear the majority of the time, and I would leave work exhausted. When I walked in the door at home, I would skip 3rd and 2nd gears and shift directly to 1st gear without realizing it. Even though I was at home, I was completely unplugged from my husband, and I rarely wanted to do things socially, and I stopped taking care of myself physically. Once I was introduced to the concept of the 5 Gears, I realized that I needed to make adjustments by letting go of some things at work and let other people take on some of my responsibilities that I had been holding onto, so that I was not constantly having to work in 5th gear and coming home so tired and stressed from work.

I also realized that I rarely shifted into 3rd gear at work for two reasons. One was that I was so overwhelmed and had to stay in 5th gear to keep my head above water, and two was that I did not want my behavior to influence anyone else to shift into 3rd gear, since there was a lot of 3rd gear going on already with other employees. I realized that I was not taking the time to connect with my team in a personal way that would make them feel valued.

Since I have been introduced to the 5 Gears, I have found healthy ways to shift between the gears when necessary and not stay in a high gear and then crash into 1st gear at the end of every day. Having the common vocabulary to communicate more effectively with my team has made a difference in our efficiency and output. It doesn't mean people don't shift into 3rd gear when they should be in 4th gear, but now I have the terminology available to positively communicate my desires to my team and become more intentional in the way I live and lead.

Imagine what life would look like if your work and life and time were a bit more balanced, not only with time management skills, but with intentional connectivity.

Intentional Work

Some of you have a hard time being present and living intentionally with other people because the pressures of tasks, coupled with your personality tendencies, cause you to get locked up in your head and stuck in 4th or 5th gear. If that is you, then here are some simple exercises you can do to become more intentional in connecting with your colleagues, co-workers, or employees:

- Give people the chance to warm up in the mornings before you barrage them with questions or projects. It is amazing what having time to grab a cup of coffee and the chance to look at their emails can do for employees' readiness to engage in the day with you.
- Stop at teammate's offices with no demands or requests but just to check in (3rd gear conversation). You might

need to get smelling salts ready as this may cause some to faint in disbelief.

- Call your team weekly for non-task-related check-ins while you are driving somewhere.
- Take someone to lunch for 3rd gear time. I used to take employees randomly and tell them ahead of time that I had no agenda other than to connect and get to know each other better. It is amazing what that little act can do.
- Establish the 5 Gears and train your teams to use the sign language to shift up or down.
- Explain 5th gear and have a sign or symbol when you are in this gear. It helps people understand what you are doing.

The results could lead to a real increase in relational capital with a number of key relationships. 5 Gears then becomes a communication tool that helps you lead more effectively, while showing what emotional intelligence looks like.

Being intentional and present allows you to be more attuned to behaviors of the people you work with. Imagine being better at identifying others' mindsets and having the ability to adjust if they are at a different level from yours.

Here are more examples from a client whose stories you have heard in earlier chapters, Ryan Underwood, who has been implementing these ways of being intentional in work settings.

- **Virtual Teams**: If you have virtual teams like we do, then you inevitably have a mix of introverts and extroverts scattered around several regions. We have been implementing 4th gear meetings via GoToMeeting with a clear agenda so that everyone feels good about getting things done. However, in the beginning, we open up with some 3rd gear check-ins, which really connect the team well before we knock out the task list.

- **Team Gatherings**: After a full day or an event some teams might do dinner together. An easy way to set the tone with intentional language is to say, "Hey guys . . . we're headed to dinner, and we'll all be in 3rd gear. No devices . . . and . . . no talking shop." Most people don't set the tone with any language and so the loudest voices would win. By holding up the three symbol, people don't feel like they are being treated like a 14-year-old instead of as a professional. The 5 Gears language allows you to address expectations much better.

- **Text Messages**: Leaders spend a lot of time with other leaders in meetings, on calls, and so on. I've got the power of the iPhone helping me shift gears and communicate with our team. I set up a "Respond with Text" message so if a team member calls and I'm either on the phone, presenting, meeting, or in another activity, I can just hit the "respond with text button." I have a pre-programmed message I can hit for our team/family that says "In 5th gear, will call you as soon as I can shift. Thanks!" Much quicker than typing all that . . . and much better than ignoring the message and not responding at all for what could be hours.

- **Using Skype**: The 5 Gears are helping us with both of these issues. I'm now intentionally working with our team to Skype and text the message, "What gear are you in?" We can easily respond to one another with 1 to 5. They know they are looking for the ideal reply of 4 and, if they receive that, can then text/Skype away. The result? The team is more available while using Skype more respectfully. And, I'm a lot less annoyed with "Are You There?" messages.

This is what it looks like to live intentionally, objectively. Set the tone, teach the objective, use shared language, and be consistent.

One of our clients has gone so far as to try and implement the 5 Gears in his relationship with his brother and father-in-law. Because this leader owns his own business, it is assumed that he can be available at any time. He often feels bad when he is in 4th and especially 5th gear and just can't talk, text, come over, and so on. He feels even worse when they try to reach out two or three times before he can call them back.

His goal is to see if he can use his growing influence to teach his family about the 5 Gears and to use it more among the clan. He has made it his goal for them all to understand what gear they are each in and begin to communicate objectively to help them grow together.

That is what being intentional looks and feels like in real life!

Let's make accidental living and accidental leadership extinct in our lives. Take the chance to begin making the changes that others would love and you would enjoy—begin to make a U-turn in the way you live your life.

14 | ⚙

Making the U-Turn— Challenge and Plan

At this point, you have reached that stage where you have all the information and can begin practicing the gears, at least in your mind. Now is the time to begin to work on the U-turn and to make the changes that actually bring new levels of influence and respect. It's time for you to experience the benefits of being present and connected.

If you are willing to accept the challenge of retooling your gears, practicing and implementing them into your life, then you will experience a deeper level of fulfillment that is rarely talked about in most leadership books or conversations. We call this applied leadership learning. And yet, before you can experience this, you need to challenge yourself.

Your Personal Challenge

This exercise will require you to have some time and a journal or piece of paper to create the makings of a leadership plan. This challenge has the potential to free you from the things you don't like and create a sense of peace in your leadership, relationships, and life. I encourage you to make this challenge personal and respond accordingly.

1. **What does it look like to be on the other side of you?** Are you willing to be honest? Are you willing to hear honest feedback? Ask two to three trusted people in your life and work what it is like for them to be on the other side of your leadership. Don't be defensive, but write their words down and let them soak in. Some of the words could be painful, maybe frustrating. Don't respond negatively, but rather, absorb them and allow this to be the starting point of becoming self-aware.

2. **What is your gear order?** Write down what it truly is, not what you want it to be. Write down your everyday schedule and the corresponding gear that you tend to be in during those times. Show some of those trusted people in your life your order to see if they agree.

3. **What gears do you drift into under stress and pressure?** Ask others or ascertain for yourself what gears you shift into under moderate stress. Get real with yourself by understanding your pressure. Where does it normally come from? List them and ask yourself if your gear order is creating any of these areas of tension. Now go further, what gear do you drift into under extreme pressure?

   Highlight the obvious gear changes that need to be made.

4. **Do you need more 1st gear or 2nd gear?** Do you need to learn how to downshift when coming home from work? What are the stories, the metaphors, and the illustrations from the previous chapters of this book prompting you to do right now?

5. **Choose your markers as trigger points to help you shift.** Do you need a marker near your home to shift to 2nd or 3rd? Use your neighborhood sign or the office door to shift your gears. Do you need to use something at work, such as a time, to trigger you to become more present and shift to the appropriate gear?

6. **Learn the gear order of those around you.** To be most effective in making the changes in yourself, it is crucial to understand the gear order of your team or spouse or friends. You set the tone of leadership by being intentional. When you can understand your tendencies and those around you, then your ability to connect goes up dramatically.

7. **Practice getting better at reverse.** Remember, respect and influence go up when we admit our mistakes and apologize. We gain ground, not lose it. Get good at apologizing appropriately and watch what happens to your relationships.

8. **Communicate the 5 Gears metaphor and language into your culture.** It is much harder to operate in the 5 Gears if those around you are unaware of the language or the concept. Teach those in your world and begin using the sign language to shape the culture and communicate more effectively.

9. **Plan to tell your future story.** In the next chapter you are going to hear a few more stories of those who have been practicing the 5 Gears. We would like to ask you to, in the future, send in your story as well as a marker for the changes that will have happened in your relationships, your work, and in yourself.

Call It, Own It, Respond, and Execute

This challenge requires that you get to the core of who you are. At GiANT, we share a tool for self-awareness called the Core Process (Figure 14.1).

- Call It—Be honest with the issue at hand. Get real and name it.
- Own It—Admit it. Know yourself and admit that the issue is yours to own.
- Respond—Lead yourself with a plan to respond to what you have owned.
- Execute—Choose a time to implement your plan of response.

We have given you the challenge. It is your time to execute.

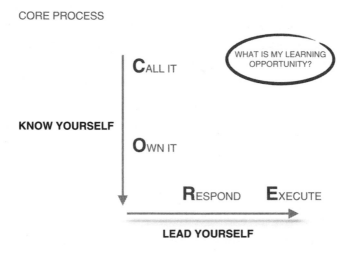

Figure 14.1   Core Process Tool

Calling it might sound something like: "I am constantly in 4th gear and I can't seem to get out of it. I wake up and check my email, talk to colleagues on the way to work, and email until I climb into bed. I think I am addicted."

Owning it would then sound like this: "It is my fault. I have not put boundaries in place at my work to let them know when I can or can't talk. I think, too, that I like being needed and have really created a monster as I am completely out of balance in my life. My reality is that my wife and kids and I are on totally different pages, and I think, in the end, it is me more than them needing to make some changes."

Responding to it might look like this: "So, I plan to reorder my gears. I realized that I need to add some real 1st gear into my life, which will help me become more organized in my mind and more healthy as I run. I am then planning to use the marker plan as a trigger to turn off. I have a sign about five miles from my house that is going to be the drop call zone. I plan on coming home connected, not distracted."

Executing would then look like this: "I am starting tomorrow. I know it will take a while for my family to feel the change, but I have already taught the 5 Gears to my team and we actually practiced using the hand signals today. I plan on teaching my wife and kids after I have done it for myself a couple of days. I am fired up to see the changes!"

That is how you take the challenge to your Core in order for you to know yourself and lead yourself. One of the leaders we work with laid out a real Core plan this way: "I have realized that my wife is one who seems to be very good at gears 1, 2, 3 and 5, while my style seems to park in 4th gear and struggle with the others." He has just called it. He is being honest and open. He goes on with this:

This has been an important clarification tool for us. I kept thinking that when my wife was in the office she was in 4th gear like me. But, what I found was that, since she is in the office roughly half the time as me, when she's in, it may look like 4th, but she's really in 5th. I was getting frustrated because I was in 4th and needed to bounce something off her, and because I "thought" she was in 4th too, I kept concluding she either didn't care or didn't like what I was bouncing. Not true. She was in 5th and I didn't get it and she couldn't get it. Now we get it better!

He just owned it. His intentional review and challenge helped him to see that he was frustrated and didn't deal with it until he owned his reality and began to help his wife see hers as well. Look how they responded to the challenge:

If I stroll over in idea mode, she now shares, "I'm in 5th gear" and I know any idea I have is futile until she shifts. How do I get her to shift? I actually schedule time and make an appointment on the calendar so we can both get in the same gear at the same time and kick ideas around.

This is a good example of how to call it, own it, respond, and execute. He was intentional about it, made a plan, and they both execute on when and how to communicate.

The 5 Gears is transferable anywhere, to any culture. We have taught it in different countries, cultures, styles of organizations, and families. In each case, we find that this leadership tool transitions powerfully through all five circles of influence—self, family, team, organization, and community.

Tim Curry, from Oxford, England, works for the National Health Service. His remarks illustrate what making a plan and executing it well look like:

I went through my diary, my family calendar, and spoke to my children about my schedule. I ended up with a picture of two weeks with 5 Gears laid over my work diary appointments, family commitments, and the family's recall of what happened to the bits in between.

The "a-ha" moment was that we had very little significant 2nd gear time. There was some good rest—sleeping later on Saturday mornings—but very little 2nd gear. At work, the 3rd gear time was squeezed and was almost always sacrificed for 4th or 5th gear. This squeezing of the gears made me think about how we change gears in a car: we depress the clutch. We literally have to press down on "drive," disengage the engine briefly, and think about which gear we are shifting to. Do I need to accelerate? Do I need to cruise? Do I need to slow down?

"Depressing the clutch" has become an intentional five-minute moment for me in between appointments and at the start of the day where I literally decide how I need to shift gears in the coming hours of the day.

It has worked well at work and my wife and I have spoken about how we make sure we make more use of our weekends to talk about how we will spend our time and what we commit to. Implementing the gears is about both lifestyle and work and it improves both.

Helping Others Mark the Changes

If you have not been able to tell, we are passionate about helping people become liberating leaders who people want to follow, but also who enjoy helping other people become liberators as well. So much so that they are willing to share their stories of transformation as we serve to inspire other leaders. We want to develop leaders worth following, not those you have to follow. In this story, Kay Lewington from Atlanta, Georgia, is one of those people who is helping others become liberators:

"I started our GiANT Core group training right before Christmas. In the second session I introduced the 5 Gears. After a brief overview we went around the table and each person identified as best they could which gear they thought there were in:

- First thing in the morning
- Middle of the day
- At night before bed

The group, as a whole, was a mixture of 1st through 5th, except for Anna, who resided in a constant 4th gear mode. Without hesitation, she knew she was stuck in 4th gear. She was taken aback at how easily she could identify herself in that context. She had no idea how she could change things as she was so consumed by the tasks of 4th gear.

We talked through some practical steps she could take, as the gear had been all consuming. For instance, she used to sleep with her cell phone on her chest to take care of any issues at work, answer emails, and so on.

She admitted that it was not healthy to be in 4th all day long and has owned it and responded with a plan. She no longer sleeps with her cell phone, which is a big step.

I think she had an unacceptable amount of reverse/ responsive mode, backing up but only to herself, taking all the blame. She has to shoulder all the responsibility anyway; as she said, being a single mother kind of puts you in 4th gear whether you want to be or not. It was imperative to teach her how to utilize the gears and put in place physical changes that she could realistically implement.

Anna's nurturer voice is often trampled and outweighed by the need and demands of the family and family life. I just had to show her a different way of managing her life and time and relationships through the gears. I asked her if her gears were the same during the week as the weekend. She responded that it depended on whether her husband had the children. If he did, she was able to utilize more of a second gear; if she had the kids, she was back at 4th gear for the entire weekend.

My suggestion to her was that she come to work in more of a 3rd gear, as she can be social with her co-workers and almost switch off from her life outside the office. She agreed and has been implementing that approach in the office. Because she is easily engrossed in her work, she is able to easily switch into 4th and 5th gears for work purposes as and when needed.

She has been in total agreement with this plan and has been happier as she has gotten comfortable with this new schedule and style of work.

We began to chart out her life and the reality of what her day is like versus her desired and achieved time (see Table 14.1). She has been working hard on implementing the gears in her life and it has become noticeable.

Table 14.1   Core Process Tool

Current		Achievable/Desired	
Time	**Gear**	**Time**	**Gear**
7am	4	7am	1
12pm	3 (4/5)	12pm	3 (4/5)
4pm	3 (4/5)	4pm	3 (4/5)
8pm	4	8pm	2
10pm	4	10pm	1

Here are the practical steps Kay's colleague Anna took to intentionally shift gears:

1. Removal of cell phone from chest to nightstand. Working on moving the phone out of the bedroom altogether.
2. Even when she is relaxing, her mind can be in 4th gear, so she will try going to the movies where she can focus on what she is watching, not using the phone, and let her mind relax
3. She used to walk, which she found therapeutic as well as beneficial exercise. Here she can find herself in 1st gear. She is going to set aside that time each evening to reintroduce this into her daily life.

When she arrives home after work, she will sit without her phone and listen to the children for 10 to 15 minutes to catch up on the day, instead of trying to listen, cook, clean, wash, tidy up, and so on, all the things she currently does as she multitasks. This will allow her to give the family her full attention in 2nd gear.

Kay concludes, saying, "Overall, I feel that Anna really welcomed this opportunity to not only have someone to listen but also to actually have some practical tools that can be applied, have phrases that mean something that can be translated into life. After all, think about it, how many times in your adult life does a person get into the weeds of your life to help.

"By getting real and finding out what gears you are actually in you can identify what you do, why you do what you do, and how you can make changes to improve your life. This process was a true eye opener to Anna and to all of us in our Core group as we processed together."

Will you take the time to get into the weeds of someone's life to help them learn how to shift and transition well in life and work? Can you go deep enough with those you lead or are around to help them get to reality and create a plan to reach their desired levels of connectivity?

Is it time to make a U-turn in your leadership and life? Have you been properly challenged in order to make a plan that could transform your personal and professional cultures in a positive way?

We believe that great leaders know how to shift into the right gear at the right time in order to be fully present and make a positive impact on others. To help people understand their gear order and transition can be a life-changing process for everyone, but you must be intentional about living it out first. You cannot give what you don't possess.

15 ⚙

What Is Your Story?

The 5 Gears is a simple metaphor that happens to be sticky, scalable, and life changing. One executive recently said, "When I first heard the gears I thought it was hokey, until it hit my reality and then they changed everything." The 5 Gears affect leaders, families, and teams, which impacts organizations and communities. We have a tool to help us when we are out of alignment and stuck in a certain gear, and now we have language that helps us transition to the right gear for the right time. The power of the 5 Gears resides in your buy-in, implementation, and ability to teach it to others.

This book is full of stories of leaders who have given us permission to share their experiences over the past few years. We know, however, that there are thousands of future stories that are yet to be written. For those of you who struggle with work/life balance, the 5 Gears are a solution. For those who have a hard time connecting with people, the stories and concepts can bring a change that is phenomenal. And for those of you who are missing your children right now because you are all-consumed by your work or responsibility, there is hope. We have struggled with these same issues. We get it. Our stories are so similar to most of yours. We are all trying to learn how to live and lead in a world full of tasks, deadlines, poor communication, expectations, busyness, and relationships. Stories help shape our reality, help to give us hope, and lead us to practical examples that can affect us for the rest our lives.

Writing Your Story

We ask people to write their personal narrative, so that they intentionally take time to put their experience into words. Somehow, the act of writing makes us think in a different way; it helps us harness our thoughts and gives them some permanence. Seeing in writing what you have experienced is powerful. With that, we want to encourage you to write your story once you have implemented 5 Gears into your work and personal life. To help get started, and because we also believe in imitation as a pathway toward transformation, here are some examples to motivate and help you as the 5 Gears bring new reality.

5 Gears Stories

Matt Keen, London, England

Guilt—we all know that feeling. You're sitting at your desk and tapping away at your computer, but your brain is fried, you're tired, and everything is starting to feel like it's too much. You know you need a break, but you're worried that other people will think that you're slacking or you think that you're letting people down so you just keep plugging away. All the time, you're getting less and less productive.

That was me 18 months ago. I was so focused on not letting people down that I really wasn't looking after myself. Guilt was a constant companion.

Then I met Jeremie and Steve. I've learned huge amounts from them both, but something that had an immediate impact on my personal well-being and the quality of my work was so simple it almost seems daft that I never worked it out myself. I was always trying to give—desperate not to let my wife, kids, friends, and colleagues down. The simple thing I started to do? Find time for 1st gear—understanding that I needed space and time alone to recharge. This approach wasn't letting people down, it would actually help me to help them more. I started carving out 30 minutes of thinking time each day in my diary to talk a walk, out of the office, and reflect. That time alone helped me to reenergize and tap into my strengths.

I now try and make sure that each week I get away from my desk and go to one of the many churches in the City of London to listen to an organ recital. It may sound strange to some of you, but that time alone, in a beautiful place, listening to beautiful music, helps me to relax, focus, and recharge. I take a pen and pad (old-fashioned, I know!) and use the hour to jot down thoughts, ideas, plans, and organize myself. This isn't something that comes naturally to me in the hurly-burly world of the modern office, but sitting alone means I can find the space to bring an order to my thoughts that I otherwise wouldn't be able to do.

I now encourage people on my team to find the ways that they can best recharge and I make sure that I publicize what I'm doing so that they know I'm practicing what I preach. Recharging makes you more productive, more creative, and happier so those around me now understand that if they want me to bring my best, then I also need that time alone to recharge. The 5 Gears has helped to create a language to express this in a way that everyone can understand.

Authors' note: It is so encouraging when a leader like Matt is vulnerable and shares what we can all recognize in our lives. This is how stories should be written—frank, powerful, and to the point.

Josh Nelson, Atlanta, Georgia

As an extrovert, I have always had lots of friends and found it very easy throughout my life to charm people and connect socially. I always knew there were going to be a few people that I wouldn't connect with, but I attributed that to the other person's insecurities around my social confidence and strong personality. Even if I had done something to damage a relationship, I was pretty good at repairing it to an amicable place. However, now looking back, these were all social or professional relationships.

Now, after having been married for 10 years and having two young children, ages five and three, and having learned about the 5 Gears, it has become glaringly obvious to me that, despite my ability to connect and relate socially, I have a tremendous inability to be present and connect intimately with them and others. To be blunt and honest, I really don't know how to be emotionally present when there is no other agenda involved or area of life for me to gain or prosper.

This has been brought to my attention now on several occasions during these early years of my boys' lives. Both my mom and my wife have expressed more than once how they desired to see me connect with my sons more intimately. To them, it looked as if my young children were an inconvenience to me and, as I honestly examined myself, I realized that I felt like they were. They did not stimulate me intellectually; they could not make me prosper, and worst of all they exposed ugliness about me that I had never known about. I remember even telling my wife, "I know I'm a bad 'baby daddy,' but I promise I'll be better once they're teenagers!"

What is this ugliness that nobody would ever want to have as a trait? And how could I, a man who could connect with and charm just about anybody throughout my entire life, who has so many friends and professional relationships, not be able to perform a simple task of being present with his own children? Even more, it shouldn't feel like a chore or a task. I actually realized that I was so bad at it that I got to the point where I dreaded holidays and weekends because it would frustrate me so much by how draining family time was.

To make it worse, people constantly rubbed this in my face without knowing it by always making comments like, "These are the best years of your life!" or "I wish they could just stay that age! Isn't it so much fun?" And all I could do was hope for a time warp to get out of this phase of life that had exposed an incompetence that I had never felt in my life. I wanted so badly to improve and get better in this area, but I honestly didn't know how to because I really didn't know what my problem was.

It wasn't until I participated in a GiANT Executive Core retreat and heard the 5 Gears presentation that I could truly begin to make some changes and grow out of this area of unconscious incompetence. Once I saw the gear order and an explanation of them, I realized that I really didn't ever go into 2nd gear. I thrived in 3rd and 4th gears, could get to 5th gear when it was really needed, under pressure or a deadline, and I liked to crash back into 1st when needing rest. However, I realized I did not do 2nd gear well at all and that is the gear that my family needed me to be in for them.

Over the next couple of months I started to really pay attention to my gears, and what I began to realize is that it wasn't that I did not have a 2nd gear to go into, it was just that I always skipped over it. I, of course, did not do this consciously, but over time I had learned to operate my life without really ever using that gear, or if I did, I transitioned out of it really quickly. So the difficult part of the last few months has been learning to "manually shift" into and stay in a gear that my automatic transmission skips over or through really quickly. However, I'm recognizing the value of this gear. In some ways, it is the most valuable of all the gears, as deep, heart-level relationships happen here. Relational trust and safety are developing here, and, ultimately, some of the things that I know I'll value greatest at the end of my life are most experienced in 2nd gear.

This gear is still, and will probably always be, my most awkward gear. I may always grind going into it and sigh coming out of it, but my hope is that, by now being conscious of my incompetence in 2nd gear, I may recognize and proclaim before God and others the need to grow and develop in this area. It is amazing the grace that others will extend to you if you just humbly recognize the struggles getting into a gear that they need you to be in, and they can see you trying on their behalf.

Authors' note: We know this feeling. Can you relate? For some of you this story hits home deeply as you, too, struggle with connecting in 2nd gear. Learning to be present is an art and a science. If you do it well it will dramatically affect those around you.

Mary Alice Higbie, Albuquerque, New Mexico

I am an introvert. My tendency is to find my energy in quiet places. Especially in times of stress I find myself going deeper into these quiet places . . . always alone, of course.

I was shocked to discover the 5 Gears and apply them to myself. What I recognized was that my "normal" was not very normal, and some parts of my "normal" were not all that healthy.

I saw that the gears I use most often are 1st and 5th gears. It has been my habit to spend at least two hours every morning in 1st gear. This time in the morning helps me focus on what is truly important and feeds my soul with that kind of food that nourishes the heart more than the body. It is the very best part of my day.

But I do have a business to run, and the last few years my work has involved more thinking, writing, and behind-the-scenes work, and less time interacting with staff and customers. When I get into working gear, it is always 5th gear. I can stay there for hours, and usually do. I am not very good in 4th gear, because distractions completely disrupt my train of thought.

It is so helpful to look at oneself from a fresh point of view. Learning the 5 Gears has taught me that I need to be with people. I need them and they need me. So I am now intentionally spending more time with others, at work and with family and friends. My husband keeps me accountable. While I continue my 1st gear time, I have modified 5th gear.

There are times when I still need a long session of 5th gear so that I can finish a project. But I am able now to be a little more balanced and the good thing is that when I am with others, I am really with them, able to focus all my attention and all my energies on them.

Understanding my tendencies has opened a window for me, helping me view my patterns and behaviors in such a way that I can make strategic changes to increase my influence and bring more balance and well-being to my life.

Authors' note: This is exactly what the gears are meant to do. Cause all of us to look at ourselves and adjust—making the changes that are needed to benefit everyone.

Austin Hodge, Atlanta, Georgia

To clarify, the 5 Gears lens helped me understand that I have an extreme natural tendency toward 1st and 5th gears, with 2nd gear making a fairly strong substitution for 1st at times.

Most of my life I've been consumed by operating at full tilt toward execution, learning, hard work, and task delivery. I have an inexorable internal compulsion toward perfectionism and a mortal fear of disappointing those I care about. Therefore, my natural tendency is to slip into 5th gear and not come up for air until the work is done, often forgetting to eat and becoming anxious about the relational burdens around me. That's why I rarely slept in high school: from five A.M. to six P.M. I had track practice, school, and then track practice again. I also took 14 AP/IB classes in high school while participating in a variety of clubs and doing my best to remain at the top of my class, so I usually didn't go to sleep until two or three A.M. when I had finished my papers, annotations, and assignments.

On the one hand, my personality draws me towards relationship, community, and a corresponding sense of guilt over relationships when they are out of balance or lacking investment. On the other hand, however, the perfectionism and sense of responsibility and achievement drives me to spurn relational touch points such as regular communication via text or phone, because they only serve to distract me from my responsibility and I have always been afraid to let anything fall through the cracks.

Through the language of the 5 Gears, I have come to understand that my 5th gear and 1st gear preference created a vicious cycle of driving me to exhaustion. Then, having no other recourse, I had to withdraw to recharge in the world in which I was most active, the internal one: one without obligations or tasks or the possibility of failing to achieve the standards and responsibilities I set for myself; one with unlimited possibilities, adventures, and marvels.

I realize now, however, that I struggled to find the middle ground in which to satisfactorily engage my need for both people and activity (mainly 2nd through 4th gears).

That's not to say I didn't enjoy life or have close family and friends. I loved my time, my upbringing, and my time at college and have experienced many joyful relationships with those I care about.

But it wasn't until college that I finally realized my gear-shifting patterns (or lack thereof) were a lot unhealthier than I thought, not to mention unsustainable for my long-term physical, mental, spiritual, and relational health.

It took many family members and friends expressing a great deal of concern in my life to convince me that I could not just keep on going as I was. One of the interesting hallmarks of this constant 5th gear activity was not only the insomnia, but the speed with which I walked. It became commonplace for me to be talking with a group of friends, only to find myself five minutes later looking 100 feet back at the group with no one around. At one point, my dad made a concerned ultimatum to pull me out of school (in the hopes of relieving stress/tension) if I did not slow down my walking pace.

It took my dad, my twin brother, girlfriends, my small group, and a powerful college ministry environment to begin softening my vicelike grip on work and worry with regard to the responsibilities and relationships in my life. Because I am fighting my natural tendencies, I am always afraid of going too far one way or another, as I believe God has called us to live the most healthy and productive life in the middle of a balanced scale.

This is still an ongoing struggle for me, but a great deal of progress has been made over the years. And with the arrival of the language and tools of the 5 Gears lens, I have gained greater understanding as well as a renewed dedication to honing the slippery, but attainable skill that is the smooth shifting of my 5 Gears (plus reverse)!

Authors' note: This young leader is amazing. He knows himself to lead himself and has incorporated the change he has needed in order to become more present and connected to those in his life while also keeping his recharge to a high level.

Joe Hill, St. Paul, Minnesota

Tenacious. Hard charging. Driven. Successful. Unbeaten. Bulletproof. Unstoppable. These are the words or phrases I would have suggested best fit my persona in my 30s and early 40s. One for each day of the week in fact. . . .

I had learned at an early age that you have to make your own breaks through hard work. "Nobody was going to be there to give a hand up to anyone who didn't have the calluses of a working man," my dad used to say. My own twist on this became my credo: "Luck was never given to anyone unwilling to work hard for it."

My life emulated this drive as a teacher, coach, school administrator, and active community member for nearly two decades. My daily routine was to wake by 4:30 A.M. to exercise and be to the office by 6:30 A.M. It was a badge of honor to be the first car in the lot and the last to leave. Lunch was for those who didn't have enough work to do, and I would regularly have meetings and community activities that brought me home in time to warm a plate of leftovers from family dinner. On the best days, I would have the chance to tuck my three kids in bed prior to crashing asleep myself while taking in the 10 o'clock news.

My mission was in full gear and I was progressing on the path of realizing it until I hit a major roadblock in March 2013. In October, prior to this disruptive awakening, I had competed in my 3rd full Ironman multisport race. I was in the best shape of my life and rocked the course! I had made an agreement with my wife that I would have a nagging sports hernia fixed in the off-season. This injury had been persistent for many years and I masked the pain through regular cortisone injections. This surgery was scheduled for February.

In the interim, I was having a very difficult time in my work role and not feeling a sense of common ground with the board of directors I worked for. The pain in my midsection coupled with my ache of dissatisfaction professionally made for a pretty miserable combination.

My elective surgery was successful and I was back on my feet a few days later. As time progressed, I was noticing a very sharp pain in my calf and beginning to notice regular bouts of dizziness and shortness of breath. One evening, while giving a public organizational performance report, I passed out briefly. My lights went out and I knew something was not right. I drove home and shared my experience with my wife. She called the ER and, while unknowingly at the time, we boarded a rail that would change our lives completely.

I was a hard-driving executive with an ego just short enough to fit through the doorway of my corner office. I ran in the red zone of 4th gear for the majority of my waking hours. Like my father, who worked harder and made unthinkable sacrifices to build his enterprise, I felt a sense of responsibility toward success at any cost in order to provide for my family. This was the success algorithm that I had memorized and now had the duty to carry the torch to pioneer and achieve, with very little time to downshift, to slow for refuel, or to genuinely connect with those who were most important to me.

My wife and I have three very active children who had countless games, concerts, and events where Mom was applauding on the sidelines as a single parent. If I was not attending an important meeting, I was being called to a social event where my presence was expected.

> 4th gear was my drug of choice and I became quite dependent upon it for my identity and my success.

From blood test to ultrasound to CAT scan to wheelchair to ICU. The doctor showed me a picture to illustrate why all the fuss. He said, "Young man," (I liked that part), "you cheated the devil." He then showed me my scan. "You have showers of blood clots in your lungs. One of them should have killed you."

Wrecked and exhausted from the pace and grind on this crazy train, I looked at my wife from the hospital bed and said, "It is time for a change . . ."

My recovery included a couple of weeks away from the office, blood thinning medication, and lots of time to reflect. Long story short: this was the experience that led to what I call my "intermission." I had not cheated the devil, I had cheated those I love the most: my wife and my kids. And it truly was time to reassess my work gear and begin to access the other gears of family, friends, and faith.

After my recovery, my wife and I felt led to put our dream house on the market and drastically downshift our lifestyle, allowing for deeper self-awareness and social awareness. This has been an incredibly rewarding second life journey and I have become more in tune with the needs of self-renewal, uncompromised time with family, and the value of personal presence within my social circles.

I still love the drive of work and have not lost the zest for success. What has changed is my own awareness of priorities. It is a yes/yes proposition of gear placement: yes to my professional ambitions and yes to my family, friends, and faith commitments. The success comes in knowing when to fully engage in the proper gear, while fully disengaging the other.

Authors' note: Your health is worth it and so is your family. When you make 4th gear your drug of choice, it is not a matter of if you will experience the consequences, but when.

Matt Hyatt, Atlanta, Georgia

The 5 Gears has truly impacted my life and my work. Here is my gear order:

1st gear is my favorite gear and easily the one that comes most naturally to me, hands down.

- I am naturally thoughtful and reflective. I don't mean kind and tenderhearted, necessarily (I wish that were always the case), I mean that I naturally find myself thinking and processing constantly in my head. I am quite comfortable and sometimes rather enjoy going for long periods of time without talking to anyone.
- I crave mental clarity. I think my mind is naturally wired to consider dozens or even hundreds of possible solutions to ideas and challenges and as I am mentally exploring each avenue toward a potential conclusion, some of them lead to other roads or even entire neighborhoods of questions and ideas to explore and consider. Before I know it, an entire morning has passed and I still haven't reached clarity on the thing that was on my mind in the first place!
- When I'm in 1st or 5th gear, I am easily annoyed by unwanted distraction, that is, any distraction that I did not

seek or create—ha! Examples include people talking near me, someone turning on a radio or TV, or even someone eating too loudly. Weird, huh? I don't *want* to feel annoyed, but I can't always control that. All I can control is my reaction to the feeling.

- Learning about the 5 Gears has helped me stop and consider whether I should change gears when I'm in first and the people around me aren't. If my wife or kids are talkative, for example, that might be an opportunity to switch to second gear and connect with them. Or if my team at the office is in a playful mood, I might switch to 3rd gear and join them for a few minutes, just for the sake of togetherness.

- Since 1st gear is my natural and favorite gear, I will seek it out when I want to recharge or relax. If my current environment is not conducive to deep thought, it's often as simple as moving to another room. During the spring and summer, I will often set up a lawn chair in the front yard and can easily spend an hour or two just watching people walk their dogs while I rest and ponder life. Going for a ride in the car has a similar effect—as long as I can avoid traffic!

- Running, working in the yard, or hiking can help me mentally resolve tough problems or come up with new ideas. For me, running is probably the quickest and best way to get into 1st gear and make progress on life's most interesting challenges. Don't get me wrong—I'm not an avid runner and I'm not particularly consistent or fast. But, when I'm at my best, a long run works wonders to provoke deep, productive thought, and it's incredibly beneficial for the body, too. I have definitely found myself so deep in thought that I can't remember the mile or two I just passed. Some of my biggest ideas and answers to my toughest problems have come to me while running.

While 1st gear is my favorite, I enjoy talking with others very much and often crave meaningful conversations. However, I'd usually rather listen and ask questions than talk.

- There's a saying that rings true for me: "Absence makes the heart grow fonder." When I'm alone on a business or photography trip and away from my family and friends for more than a day or two, I often can't wait to get back to reconnect with people. In fact, I think I prefer to have a little 2nd gear time every four or five waking hours. When I'm alone for more than a day or two, I begin to really look forward to getting back to the important people in my life.
- 2nd gear is critical, but a little bit tends to go a long way with me! Usually an hour or two of 2nd gear is enough to refuel, then I'm ready to get back into 1st or 5th.
- When I'm in 2nd gear, I prefer to listen and ask questions, rather than talk. Still, I can be quite talkative, if the mood strikes me. This is especially true when I've satisfied my curiosity about the topic of discussion and someone asks my opinion. I enjoy sharing my conclusions, once I've worked them out in my head—ha!
- Like most people, I also enjoy talking about myself, but typically only after I've been able to listen and ask questions first. I think it is that I want to be sure that whatever I say will be relevant and impactful to the person or people I'm talking to. I don't enjoy talking just for the sake of hearing my own voice.
- 3rd gear is my least favorite and, particularly in the company of strangers, can be very uncomfortable for me.
- Learning about the 5 Gears helped me recognize the importance of other gears for many of my closest friends and family. For example, some of my favorite people are extroverts and many of them enjoy 3rd gear very much. Knowing that helps me to tolerate a party or social gathering, even when it would otherwise be uncomfortable for me.

- I rather enjoy a party or dinner with lots of people I know well, but that's probably cheating a little bit, since I will probably spend a little 2nd gear time with several different people at such a gathering.
- 4th gear is tolerable, but not my favorite. Still, I spend a lot of time there.
- At work, 4th gear is my *modus operandi*. As the CEO of my firm, Rocket IT, I like to hear what's happening in the business and I want to remain accessible to my team, so I spend a great deal of my time with my office door wide open and mentally "open to interruption."
- 5th gear is what happens when mental clarity has been reached.
- I find I am most productive once I've had enough time in 1st gear to figure things out. Once an idea has been formed or a conclusion reached, I quickly become anxious to put it into action. That often means documenting the idea by typing it out or putting it in a spreadsheet, sending an email, or otherwise sharing it with someone.
- Like 1st gear, 5th gear is a favorite and I can easily allow a half day to go by without even noticing. I love being in a productive groove!

Authors' note: As you read the stories of others, we hope they inspire you to think deeper and more intentionally than ever before as you journey on the road to being a leader worth following.

It's Your Turn

Now it's time for you to write your story, to join the dialogue of leaders wanting to be present and more connected. We have made it easy for you. Go to www.5gears.me and enter your story. The directions are on the site.

More importantly, implement the 5 Gears as you learn how to shift gears, create markers as trigger points, and communicate to those around you objectively to become more present as a leader and as a person. If you will commit to being in the right gear at the right time, then your chances of experiencing better relationships will go up exponentially as well.

The 5 Gears is a lifestyle. Do it well and experience a life that is fulfilling and the influence that goes along with someone becoming a person that others want to emulate. It will take your self-awareness and intentional willpower to learn to shift well and lead others into their own personal breakthrough.

Give everyone a gift—you. Be present with those in your life and those that you lead. When you do, you will watch your influence thrive and your respect flourish. We wish you all the best in that endeavor!

Transformational Leadership Resources

If you would like more information about the 5 Gears and how to apply them in your life or would like to add your story, visit www.5gears.me. You can also find out more information about the 5 Gears Master Class as well.

Numerous organizations have benefited from implementing the 5 Gears in their companies. If you would like to arrange a workshop for your team or organization, contact hello@giantworldwide.com

If you would like more leader resources, including workbooks, exercises, videos, or tools, then contact www.giant worldwide.com/blog.

If you would like to be apprenticed to learn how to create a system to change your culture and build a team of all-stars, take a look at www.executivecore.info or contact hello@giantworldwide.com to schedule a conversation.

Finally, you can utilize www.jeremiekubicek.com for personal reflection and learning and www.giantworldwide.com for company information.

About GiANT
Worldwide

We build GiANTs. A GiANT is a type of leader who has become secure, confident, and humble in order to build high-functioning teams and to transform their leadership cultures.

We do this through a revolutionary process that is simple and scalable. By establishing a common language through visual tools we apprentice leaders to become self-aware as they become leaders worth following and help them create a long-term leadership system that truly works. We focus on raising the level of leadership throughout the entire organization, not just the top 10 percent, while creating a focus on long-term organizational health.

Our specialty includes:

1. Teaching a common language that 90 percent of an organization can utilize.
2. Implementing visual tools that shape culture and enhance leadership growth.
3. Inserting an apprenticeship process that blows away the traditional leadership development programs with a system that impacts culture for a decade.
4. Focusing on individual transformation rather than on information transfer alone. We teach self-awareness that

spreads throughout teams to produce secure, confident, and humble leaders.

5. Serving clients in agile and relevant ways to fit the fast-paced, task-oriented work world. We truly work around the world with offices in London, Atlanta, and Oklahoma City.

To find out more information go to www.giantworldwide.com.

Acknowledgments

We would like to thank the following people for their partnership and friendship as we have been implementing the 5 Gears in our lives and writing it for many others to benefit:

- Thank you to our families for your dedication and for putting up with our travel and constant rambling about new tools, metaphors, and concepts to help others. Thanks for allowing us to be us.
- Thank you Amy Norton for your great eye for editing and for your partnership in GiANT.
- A big thank you to Mike Oppedahl, Justin Westbrooks, Hunter Hodge, and Austin Hodge for your leadership and partnership in building out an infrastructure to literally change the world!
- To all the GiANT Worldwide partners and senior associates in the United States and in the United Kingdom—we want to thank you! Mark and Jill Herringshaw, Brian Willamson, Elizabeth Paul, Jane Fardon, Dan Frey, Joe Hill, Maria Guy, Amy Norton, Scott Wiethoff, Dan Huckins, Debbie Correa, Don Peslis, Jay Sampson, Chris Ediger, Eddie Backler, Matt Hyatt, LV Hanson, Chad Miller, Tyler Van Epps, Tim Curry, Peter Wyngaard, Davidson Brooks, Ben Ambuehl, Bill DeMarco, Toby

Bassford, Jeff Dorman, Andy Eun, SunAwh Park, Kathy Hegelson, Tom Nebel, Jeff Raymond, Josh Nelson, Tom Cole, Kevin Hart, Nataliya Higbie, Susan Cumbus, EJ Lee, and Jared Humphries.

- To our future associates—thank you for jumping into the water. What fun we will have together.
- Chris Ferebee has been a rock star as well. Thank you for your hard work.
- To Jeff Lamkin, Kevin Bailey, Brandon Hutchins, and Matthew Myers, thanks for believing in us!
- Thank you to Pat Lencioni, Amy Hiett, Henry Cloud, and Jon Gordon for your friendship and counsel over the years!
- We have really enjoyed our partnership with John Wiley & Sons. Thanks to Shannon, Matt, Liz, and the team for all your hard work!
- A special thanks to our clients for allowing us to be us in helping you be you. Special shoutouts to Andrew Dahl, Heather Ladwig, John Cotterell, and Matt Keen for your early feedback on the process.
- Thanks to the wider GiANT family for your partnership—GiANT Capital, GiANT Partners, GiANT Experiences, and GiANT Impact.
- Lastly, thank you, the reader, for being open to becoming more present. Have fun implementing the 5 Gears and growing your influence!

Index